GENIUS SIMPLE BRANDING™

How a 1-Page Branding Map Can Revitalize Your Business

Andy Cleary | Cody Cleary

Logos, Book Cover & Text Design by Cindy Kroeger

Genius Simple Branding™ *Unlock Working Magic > Light Up*
Sales
By
Andy Cleary
Cody Cleary, MBA
Logos, Book Cover & Text Design by Cindy Kroeger
Thumbnails by John Stavola and Cindy Kroeger

ISBN 978-0-557-06572-1
Manufactured in USA
Published and Distributed by Lulu Publishing
Produced by Genius Simple Online

2560 Sheridan Blvd., Suite 4
Denver, CO 80214
303-433-1616
www.Orbit-Design.com
www.GeniusSimpleBranding.com
www.BrandingMap.com
www.GeniusSimpleDesign.com
Genius Simple Branding™
Branding Map Process®
Orbit Design™ *Genius Simple Branding*

"Until you understand who you are, success will be difficult."
— Og Mandino, *Millionaire and Author of*
"The Greatest Salesman in the World"

*"In my experience, simplicity has always been entirely more
effective than complex brand development and communication,
so a robust, authentic strategy is always better."*
— James Leipnik
Canon
Chief of Communications and Corporate Relations

*"Anyone can make things complicated. Keeping it simple takes
a genius."*
— Roswell
Orbit's Brander-in-Chief

Contents

The Genius Simple Branding Map™
The Ultimate Competitive Advantage

Preface

Dear Reader,

Every concept in this book was gleaned through finger-on-the-pulse interaction with clients over 29 years, by branders and designers, who often worked way beyond normal business hours to meet unforgiving "drop deadlines." You can be assured that each principle has been fired in the crucible of an active branding design studio helping real clients, frequently in survival mode, to meet actual, primary sales objectives.

The Promise Your Company Makes

Branding is the unique promise your business makes and keeps to its customers. You may think that keeping one promise is easy to do. It is not. It takes the self discipline of a Zen master, the focus of a rocket scientist, and the wisdom of a guru to accomplish this seemingly simple task. Why? Because there is an overwhelming temptation in the world of business to complicate, obfuscate and confuse.   But the most successful businesses in the world have one thing in common. They are monomaniacal in keeping their Branding Promise to their customers … to their crowd. What's more, they are constantly building on that promise and using it to better support and inspire their crowd. They do it automatically, systematically, compulsively. Ultimately, they become one with their crowd, anticipating needs and wants because they are their own.

Every Branding Promise has its own rules – that's why there are no universal laws in branding. Every Brand needs to influence and create a feeling of trust in the customer – that's why every purchase is emotional.

When a business operates from core values, gets everyone on the same page and follows a Branding Promise that is valuable to a specific crowd, it is a beautiful thing to watch. Deals fall into place, customers seemingly come out of nowhere, the whole company inside and out is in sync. All the hard work is paying off and the marketing comes alive. Suddenly it is your company that is on a roll. And you are getting exponential results. Only a genius like you could keep your brand that simple.

Brand well and prosper,

Andy Cleary

Cody Cleary

Declaration
You Are the Brander for Your Company

You are the brander…

When push comes to shove; when you need to close that important deal – if you are not "feeling" your own brand, your customers, prospects, even your own staff never will.

You are the brander…

Know who you are, what you stand for, who your crowd is, where you are going and how you are going to get there. Get it down on paper – ONE PAGE. That is the Genius Simple Branding Map process®.

You are the brander…

Your task is to connect your core value with value to the customer. That is a Branding Promise. When you make your branding promise be sure to keep it.

You are the brander…

Give the gift of a clear Brand and fresh buzz to your sales people. You will be amazed at the difference in their performance.

You are the brander...

Keep your company "on Brand". If you have hodge podge marketing materials and inconsistent sales messaging you will confuse your customer. Confusion is the enemy of sales.

You are the brander...

Your brand is the oil well of your future.

You are the brander...

Every company; you as a leader; your employees; your customers; all have a certain genius. Take off the lids!

You are the brander.

GENIUS SIMPLE BRANDING™

How a 1-Page Branding Map Can Revitalize Your Business

Andy Cleary | Cody Cleary

WHY
GENIUS
SIMPLE
BRANDING

gobbling up sales

What is the Branding Magic Coke® and Nike® have?

We frequently poll our Genius Simple Branding™ seminar attendees and ask them to recite their company's mission statement. More often than not, no one in the room can do this. We ask entrepreneurs and marketing directors if they follow their marketing plans – the ones that even have one are lucky if they know where they filed it. We ask about that bulging binder of marketing research – how thick is the layer of dust on it? We hear many marketers comment that they are somewhat embarrassed by their logo. We hear about marketing materials that were pretty but sit unused in storage because they are outdated, inaccurate or were useless the day they were printed. There is nothing more common than the story of the neglected web site that never gets updated or visited. Countless viable ideas are erased from business white boards every day. And finally, we listen to salespeople at odds with marketing people, blaming each other for missed opportunities with customers old and new.

For companies large and small, what a gigantic waste of time and energy.

But we have repeatedly observed over the last 26 years, that the companies both large and small, that bypass the problems above, that go on a roll, are gobbling up sales, achieving their objectives, creating their own marketing space with all the pieces magically falling into place have, had one thing in common – a Genius Simple™ Brand.

Beginning with the End in Mind

The first and easiest obstacle is purely semantic – let's remove the word "marketing" from the discussion. Marketing is a beautiful word – it calls to mind "bringing to market," a great place where mankind's goods, services and ideas are exchanged. But marketing, as it is used in business today, is a separator, a touchy-feely buffer, a would-be umbrella and in most cases has totally lost its meaning. Does branding drive marketing, is branding a function of marketing, does marketing drive sales … somehow marketing always gets in the way, separating branding from sales.

The primary purpose of branding is to improve sales.

Branding work always begins with the end in mind, i.e. sales. If this focus can be maintained, you will not stray into the wasteland of Fuzzy Image Branding (FIB) and you will stay on track with Rubber to the Road Branding (RTR). Both approaches are unlimited creatively. But RTR stays directly attached to the task at hand.

What is Branding?

Here is a dictionary definition of a brand:

rubber to the road branding

> "A brand is a product, service or business that has established a relationship with the customer. A brand creates expectations about what a customer will experience."

Here is an old, but helpful definition to remember: "A Brand is a shortcut you create in your customer's head."

Finally:

> ◦ Branding weighs nothing yet it is the most valuable substance in the world: It is the essential grease and glue of business.

All three of these definitions are accurate. Though the third one reads like a riddle, it is the one that is most helpful in brand development.

Genius? I'm no genius.

"People who boast about their IQ are losers."
— Stephen Hawking, Physicist

fire in the belly

Cellist Yo-Yo Ma once said, the most proficient and renowned musicians are not necessarily those who outshone everyone as youths, but rather those who had "fire in the belly". Is there anything so common as the underachieving genius parking cars for a living? Most experts agree on the "Ten Year Rule:" People who invest a huge amount of work in one focused area – be it a sport, an academic subject or a business – for a period of ten years are most likely to earn the genius label and success by whatever measure.

Anders Ericsson, professor of psychology at Florida State University in Tallahassee, who has studied genius comments: "(Genius) happens because some external things line up so that a person of good intelligence can put in the sustained, focused effort it takes to achieve extraordinary mastery. These people don't necessarily have an especially high IQ, but they almost always have very supportive environments, and they almost always have important mentors. And the one thing they always have is this incredible investment of effort."

This is the type of genius that is able to create a great brand. In business, the company with the iconoclastic, counterintuitive knowledge gleaned from years of experience, is the one most able to separate itself from the competition. There is always a chunk of savvy hidden in these companies. As branders, we always strive to unlock this genius, this hard won magic, and then help sell it systematically.

iconoclastic, counterintuitive knowledge

Simple? Business is complex and difficult.

"Simple does not mean simple minded and certainly does not mean easy to do."

– Roswell

Brands must be simple or they simply don't work. Your brand must be easy to understand and remember. The great brand offers just the right crowd an easily digestible suggestion of genius or distilled magic.

Unfortunately, it is nearly impossible to keep a brand simple.

Keep it simple stupid – the old **KISS** principle applies to branding with one profound adjustment: After years of working in branding, we have found it takes a veritable genius to keep a brand simple.

We (including the authors of this book) are often our brand's worst enemy. We can have a marketing meeting and do more damage to our brand than a hundred competitors would do over ten years. The grass is always greener and we water down our brand to "scale" up for a wider audience. We decide to create a new brand extension or sub-brand. We scrap the best parts of our "old" brand just when our customers are "getting" our message. We get attracted to the latest "bright shiny object" (BSO) in the world of marketing. We let a focus group or the competition dictate where we are going. Many of the leading brands in the world are guilty of these sins, including the #1 brand in the world.

The best companies are obsessively, relentlessly genius simple. The best brand builder in the world is Coca-Cola.® They long ago won the cola wars – Pepsi® remains competitive with a savvy purchase of Frito Lay®. Coke's main problem is that they have run out of planet. The Coca-Cola® brand is perennially ranked #1 in the world with brand equity currently valued at $69.3 billion. Write that check and you get no trucks, no manufacturing plants, not even a free pass to the World of Coke in Atlanta. That figure is how much their brand, and brand only, is worth. It is the largest item on Coke's balance sheet. Yet the Branding Promise for Coke can be summed up in one sentence. The entire brand can be mapped out on a page. The basic logo hasn't changed since the late 1800s. Later, as we look at Coke's influence on the Genius Simple Branding™ model, you will see what can happen when a company is able to stay relentlessly Genius Simple.

Reality: Have you done your branding homework?

I don't care if the person on the other end of the line wants our firm to design a business card or a complete sales action system ... the first question I ask is: "Have you done your branding homework?" What I'm asking is: have you taken the time to examine the value of your own product or service and how it will work in the marketplace. Do you know how to create positive buzz? Without understanding your own brand, distilling a message and figuring out a go-to-market strategy, how can you create excitement? Without a branding map you are doomed to the same old same old:

We Have High Quality + Lower Price = Customer Yawning

Everyone is selling high quality and low price. Important? Yes. Assumed? Also Yes. Every company has branding by default. You don't have to lift a finger. Branding exists in the minds of your customers and prospects. Branding is what people say about your company when you are out of the room. You may think that if you work hard and produce quality products or services, then branding will take care of itself. This is called "passive" branding and can be very dangerous. A good reputation is a hundred times harder to maintain without proactive branding. Make one mistake and negative buzz will quickly fill that brand vaccum you left. Suddenly you have the business disease known as the "Angel Complex" where you must be perfect at everything.

Let's take an extreme example: Imagine that one day a customer went into McDonald's® and upon being served a Happy Meal® promptly threw a fit because it wasn't gourmet quality and served on fine china. This never happens. Why? Because McDonald's® has done their branding homework. Their core buzz is in your ears. Your kids love their "Happy Meal". You love their super quick service, clean facilities, play space, and their good works - The Ronald McDonald House for parents of hospitalized children. Their brand's core buzz displaces any negative buzz. If you have done your branding homework here are some items you might know:

If you live in a semi-civilized country above earth's surface, you know that McDonald's® willfully compromises on their food quality in order to deliver you a consistent product with super quick turnaround. When I hear that someone has a good reputation in their industry, I know that they did their branding homework.

If you have done your branding homework here are some items you might know:

Angel Complex

> You know your Branding Promise (it's less than seven words) and so does everyone in your company from stockroom to boardroom.

> You know your "handle" and your full name and your slogan and what they do and how to protect them.

> You know what your company stands for.

> You know the "ideal crowd(s)" your company aims to work with.

> You know your company's position in the marketplace.

> You know your company's "salty soundbite".

> You know your company's core values, relevant benefits, personality, and themes.

> You know what your company is trying to be best at.

> You know how your company is going "overboard" to underscore your branding.

> You know how to introduce new customers to your brand.

> You know your company's approved branding icons.

> You know what your BWAK (buzz worthy Apathy Killer) is.

> You know what your credibility kicker is.

> You know what your branding icons are.

> You know what your intellectual property (IP) is.

BWAK
(buzz worthy apathy killer)

If you know the above, then congratulations. You have a fully developed brand to support your sales.

And you may proceed – your branding homework, i.e. your Branding Map is done.

(All others please keep reading, we will help you build your own Branding Map.)

Brand Equity and Return on Investment (ROI)

"Business owners set all their hope on the big payoff as their end game," comments Jim Muelhausen, founder of CEO Focus. "Often, nearly 80 percent of the time, it's a distinct disappointment."

One of the major bad surprises is that prospective buyers are interested in just one thing: <u>your brand's attachment to your client base</u>. All of your hard assets are usually readily replaceable, fully depreciated or just plain worthless. Employees and software are more often than not replaceable if push comes to shove. Even past profitability is suspect as brand strength determines whether or not profitability can survive the sale of the company.

Therefore, your brand, that technically lives in your client's head, is all that a buyer will see as motivation to shell out hard-earned cash. And if your brand, as unprotected intellectual property, exists primarily in the owner/founder's head, then the brand is even less valuable.

One of Muelhausen's alternatives to the *big payoff* approach is what he calls "Emeritus" status, which means "continue building your brand until it can provide you with continuing income and freedom, as you take a reduced, yet impactful 'emeritus' role in the company. Never sell your company."

> *"A brand is not a periodic campaign – a brand drives growth over the life of the company."*
>
> — *Roswell*

Branding is far superior to quality in driving sales and building company value. Going back to the McDonald's® example: Is the McDonald's® hamburger, even their signature Big Mac,® the highest quality burger in your neighborhood or any neighborhood? Obviously not, but it is most likely the best selling hamburger. McDonald's® branding is about clean, fast food service for families with kids. Their famous brand adds about $25 billion to McDonald's® value as a company.

⟩ The Real World Value of Branding

Each year the top brands in the world are rated by a large foundation known as Interbrand (interbrand.com). Here are the world's Top Ten Brands as of this writing.

1. Coca-Cola® $70.4 billion
2. IBM® $64.7
3. Microsoft® $60.8
4. Google® $43.5
5. GE® $42.8
6. McDonald's® $33.5
7. Intel® $32
8. Nokia® $29.5
9. Disney® $28.7
10. Hewlett-Packard® $26.9

Of this list, none wind up in the top ten in advertising spend. Strong brands always save in advertising costs, especially small businesses.

Branding: The Ever Appreciating Asset

Going beyond brand equity, how does a brand increase the value of your company? There are three primary ways:

First, branding gives your company "sustainability" – the basis for a solid independent existence. How can a succession plan work effectively without an autonomous brand?

At the very least, good branding consists of a Branding Promise, branding icons, an Apathy Killer, credibility kicker, icons and intellectual property all in a thematic package. These should be congruent with the values, character and culture of your company. All marketing, advertising and PR should stay "on brand." Clever ad campaigns may come and go but your brand lives on. Charismatic salespeople can come and go but your brand lives on. You, the owner or marketing director, can come and go but your brand lives on. Branding is the backbone of your company's sustainability.

Second, branding provides a victorious cycle (as opposed to a vicious cycle) comparable to compound interest. If your sales efforts stay "on brand," then you are cumulatively building up critical mass in the market until you reach the "tipping point" where your sales begin to delightfully snowball. In turn, the increase in client base creates a more powerful brand and so the cycle goes on. Branding is the true basis for viral sales and always gives you a lottery ticket for sales growth.

Third, a cohesive, vital brand makes your company more attractive to what we call "trailers." You can shape your brand to a particular "crowd" but customers are your crowd if <u>they</u> decide to be your crowd. The most famous example of crossover selling to trailers is Tommy Hilfiger's nautically themed clothing line finding unexpected popularity among the hip-hop nation. To his credit and advantage, Hilfiger embraced his "trailers." Everyone finds a well put together brand interesting and attractive.

The New Branding Quad

The U.S. is in a well-documented transition from a manufacturing economy to an information economy to an economy of ideas. Futurists are clocking the speed at which information is multiplying and are predicting after three years information will double every 72 hours. Branders, both inside and outside of future companies, are charged with the task of tapping into this huge reserve and converting it to commercially viable fuel.

> *"Branding is the new oil well of the future."*
> — ***Roswell***

Going forward through the future and the next section – the Genius Simple Branding Map™ – there are four simple branding guidelines that will keep recurring:

> *Follow Your Branding Promise*

> *Keep Your Finger on the Pulse*

> *Selling = Branding + Outreach*

> *Support and Inspire Your Crowd*

This Branding Quad represents a foundation for selling in the faster, sleeker, more demanding economy of the future.

THE
GENIUS
SIMPLE
BRANDING
MAP™

GETTING ON THE SAME PAGE

"Until you understand who you are, success will be difficult."
— **Og Mandino,** *Millionaire and Author of*
"The Greatest Salesman in the World"

What is a Genius Simple Branding Map™?

Sales and so-called marketing efforts, in even the best of companies, is like herding kittens. People and departments get temporarily enthusiastic, wander around, lose their place, return and then get lost again. The CEO gets panicky over a bad month, so an advertising campaign is hastily launched.

The Genius Simple (GS) Branding Map™ is designed to keep everyone literally on the same page, aware of what they are doing and why. The specific purpose of the map is to find "True North" for all of your marketing in the form of a Branding Promise. In addition, your trade names, positioning, elite eight, branding icons, Apathy Killer, Credibility Kicker, intellectual property, theme and signature piece are committed to paper. The GS Branding Map™ helps build the foundation for a solid selling system that consistently and persistently builds your business. The map of your brand fits on one sheet. Unlike mission statements and strategic planning, your Branding Map™ is easy to remember and act upon.

Finding True North – Your Branding Promise

If you go beyond traditional classroom marketing – the academic model, i.e. research, mission statements, business plans – and you study the best branding and selling systems in the world, you will discover the Branding Promise. The beauty of the Branding Promise is its simplicity. It must be expressed in less than seven words so that everyone in the organization can clearly understand and memorize it. The Branding Promise must contain the essential benefit that you passionately and unvaryingly provide to your customer. It is the heart of your branding and the soul of your sales effort. It constitutes the "single takeaway" so well known in advertising.

The most successful brands in the world, from Coca-Cola® beginning in 1886 to Dell Computers® founded in 1984 were built around very simple … genius simple … Branding Promises. We have found that after setting their Branding Promise some businesses discover for the first time what they really do, and are able to easily explain what they do to their clients. For the first time everyone – prospects, clients, staff, and vendors – are all on the same page.

find
"True North"

Below are eight shorthand "rules" for developing a strong Branding Promise.

1. Seven words or less. One word is fine.

2. Start with "You get…" no matter what.

3. Internal for company – slogan is for outside (clients, prospects).

4. Eliminate the obvious – suggest, do not explain.

5. Something you could be best at – doesn't have to make sense.

6. Double meanings are welcome.

7. No corporate speak.

8. What do you stand for?

"The big shots are only the little shots who keep shooting."
– Christopher Morley

> **Your Branding Promise Should Express What Your Company Stands For.**

Your Branding Promise should suggest, not explain, what your company is about. It is needed to help your leadership, your staff and even strategic partners recognize easily what you are most serious about delivering to your clients. The idea is to secure quick comprehension and "buy in" on what you are trying to do.

A Branding Promise is not a slogan in most cases. They have differeing roles. A Branding Promise is a bridge from your primary value to value for your customer. The job of a slogan is to "salt" your customers interest.

Companies that neglect developing a Branding Promise will focus on a moment in time or an anecdotal experience and create a hodge-podge of marketing pieces and messages. Of course, there are some brands that can thrive on the moment – fads like the "Pet Rock" have their 15 minutes of fame but the stronger, more established companies, regardless of size, are focused on a long lasting brand. They use their branding as a means to drive growth over an extended period of time. A moment can show a sales spike but that moment will inevitably pass; a brand can live on and on.

Be sure your core buzz is based on your Branding Promise and not on a collection of spontaneous "marketing ideas." Your Branding Promise should provide "True North" for your branding and allow you to build consistent, purposeful messaging; magnetic branding icons; an irresistible Apathy Killer; a rock solid credibility kicker; and consistent, congruent marketing tools.

The Power of a Branding Promise

A young computer geek built his computer empire of 46,000 employees on one word – Accountability. He started his computer company from the trunk of his car while still a college student. His idea was to eliminate the middle man, and as the retailer, he would be accountable to every single customer – as if he was still by himself selling on a one-to-one basis. Even early on, he wanted the customer to see no difference between buying a computer from the trunk of his car or from a $20 million company.

His Branding Promise, "Accountability," was huge for him. He selected his board of directors and shipping room personnel based on their personal accountability. It worked on all levels of the company. The human resource department loved it. They had an extremely clear vision of who should be working for them. If you had a bevy of computer whizzes to select from, the deciding factor was who had demonstrated more accountability in his or her life.

At one point the company was hiring 150 people a week. The clear commitment to the simple and memorable Branding Promise made it possible for people to get up to speed immediately.

hiring 150 people a week

Imagine the challenges of the Research and Development Department. Everyone in the company is obsessed with accountability. As a result, they decided that their machines had better be bullet proof. Previously, the computer industry standard was to start up and "burn in" computers on a random test basis. Their engineers decided to take their Branding Promise to an extreme. They decided to burn in every single computer that went out the door. They color coded all connections and made each computer extremely easy to set up. The result had a viral effect in the industry.

You no longer needed a computer firm to "set up" your computer and get it running right. Anyone could do it with consistently positive results. In a competitive, low margin commodity industry, this one word Branding Promise took them to the top of the computer manufacturing world. You probably already guessed that this brand is Dell® Computers?

> *"Working magic – the gradual accumulation of little pieces of counterintuitive savvy you gain through experience every day – that is what makes you a business genius."*
> — ***Roswell***

> *"Your greatest competition is not your competition. It is indifference."*
> — ***Harry Beckwith,*** *Selling the Invisible*

Meet Martha

Once upon a time a young hotshot newspaper feature writer decided to seek his fortune as an advertising copywriter. He managed to get hired by a small advertising department. One day, very suddenly, a picture of an attractive professional woman with a discerning look was thrust in front of his face. "You are no longer writing for a newspaper. This is your new sweetheart and I want you to tape her picture right over your typewriter. From now on, all the copy you write is going to be a personal letter to ... Martha." Street Hale stood up, smiled at his last minute name selection, took a deep drag on his pipe and observed the effect of his directive on his rookie copywriter. The rookie sat there and thought about how much his boss looked like Norman Rockwell. The rookie reluctantly taped the picture of "Martha" onto the

orange fabric of his modern cubistic cubicle above his beloved electric Smith Corona.

"Furthermore," Street intoned, "when you finish each page of ad copy, I want you to read it out loud to Martha, and see how she reacts." Now this sounded downright humiliating to the young copywriter. He decided he would comply with his boss' wishes but only over lunch when everyone was gone. But gradually he noticed two things that were odd.

First, Martha worked; that is, her enigmatic stare actually spoke to him loud and clear. She said, "This is fluff, do I really need to know that, check that fact, toss this and start over, or even, that's pretty good, turn it in to Street." The second odd thing he noticed was that the other copywriters, the editor, the layout artists and even Street himself were reading at a barely audible level to various Martha images on their walls.

Thirty years later, the fifth version of "Martha" hangs over the new Compaq® laptop in the rookie's successful business. The lesson of Martha is that you are always selling to one single human being and since your brand lives inside her head – well you better get inside her head or you will be communicating – in words or images – irrelevant junk. You may be doing a multimillion dollar campaign for a demographic that includes most of the planet but ... if it doesn't work on the level of one single individual, it will not work at all.

Over the years this intriguing woman changed and there was a lot more for the rookie to learn from her. Martha became busy and time started to evaporate out of her life. As a professional, wife and a mother, her attention span for the rookie's marketing messages shrank down to 23 seconds or less.

Finally the rookie had to struggle to get her attention with a salty headline and unforgettable images. Martha is smart and she still continued her habit of reading but she no longer read the rookie's copy – she scanned it. So now every paragraph has a subhead. Bulleted copy has taken over and even the bullets have two or three topic words in bold to summarize the bulleted copy. And where has Martha's trust gone? She's been fooled by clever marketers and her guard is always up. She doesn't have time or money to waste. Now things are interactive and Martha likes the choice and immediacy of interacting with her vendors. She will let you know if she's unhappy.

salty headline

Martha is not a selfish woman but the question on her lips is, "What's in it for me?" So even after you get through Martha's defense mechanism, you wind up at Martha's heart, which for marketers is made of stone. The rookie is used to this fact about Martha and he knows that helping Martha buy anything – no matter how logical it seems – is an emotional decision. The rookie knows that his job is to chip away at that heart of stone bit by bit, marketing message by marketing message. And he has learned that the way to Martha's heart is through affinity groups – people she knows and trusts. He knows he can never take her for granted. He must go that extra mile to network with her, keeping in touch with her needs and wants and adjust his brand accordingly.

⟩ The Ultimate Realization about Martha*

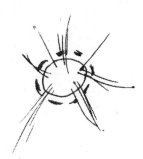

But the ultimate realization about Martha that struck the rookie one day was that suddenly Martha had stopped asking the definitive sales question: "What's in it for me?" Instead she was asking, "Is it me?" Martha and most other consumers were increasingly searching for self actualization through brands. What's more, the feeling was getting as strong as institutional allegiances such as school, religion, sports and ethnic identification. There are Maybelline® or L'Oréal® women, Ford® or Chevrolet® men, Nike® or Adidas® boys, American Girl® or Barbie® girls, Blackberry® or I-Phone® executives, Microsoft® or Apple® computer users … and so on ad infinitum. Keeping a finger on the pulse of Martha's world became paramount – the rookie listened even closer to what the silent Martha had to say.

We have all become Marthas, vigilante decision-makers, fending off unwanted offers and salespeople. You have a very small window to fit your branding message into. The Branding Promise is permanent, True North for your brand. The Apathy Killer is the expression of your Branding Promise gone hyper. It can be permanent or temporary, but it helps you to consistently break through Martha's apathy and fly through those brief windows to make that essential connection. Your prospects are inundated with paper and electronic marketing messages seeping into every corner of their attention spans.

*See pg. 121 for "Covering Martha's Bases" and "Martha's Buying Outreach System".

The same rules apply to you, the small business owner and IBM®. In any marketing environment, you have 23 seconds or less to make a connection with your client.

Why "Customer-Centered" Branding Is a Waste of Time

The "customer-centered" approach to branding is often touted in marketing circles as sacred, just as the adage that "the customer is always right" has held sway for many years right down to today. On these issues a "yes, but" approach seems wise.

Surprise me!

Customer-centered branding" argues that you should get permission and validation from the customer before developing your branding concepts and value propositions, i.e. find out from the customer what is needed and then meet that need. This sounds very logical … politically correct … what could be better? However, in reality, customer-centered branding and marketing is the road to mediocrity.

Any vital business lives in a robust world that often constitutes just a tiny fraction of the end user's (customer's) life. As a customer, I want to know what's possible from people who eat, sleep and drink their product all day long. Surprise me! For instance, you and I as customers have no clue as to what the next great step for the cell phone is. We all expect, and rightfully so, that the obsessed, inspired people in the cell phone industry will take care of this with no effort on our part. Don't ask me what I want in a survey or focus group – I might want a cell phone that washes my car, what do I know? Show me your innovation and let me be the judge as to whether you actually improved the customer experience for me. I will applaud your efforts with cash.

As a brander, I look for inspired business ideas because people buy on emotion. Sales people know that customers only resort to logic if they can use it to justify buying what they really want. Customers know a valuable innovation or brilliant benefit when they see it.

Salespeople, and anyone in the trenches with customers (hopefully the executive staff), are the best source of branding. They ought to be in sync with your company's "crowd" or better yet, they should be elbow-to-elbow crowd members. Tony Hawk is around 40 years old, but he has a skateboard complex in his yard. He is still a quintessential part of his crowd. Subscribe to his e-blast, not because you know or care which end of a skateboard is up, but because he is such an enduring brander. You will see that Tony is still a genuine member of his skateboard crowd. I'll bet Tony plays correct hunches about what his crowd wants. I'll bet Tony never makes kids fill out questionnaires about their likes/dislikes and price points. I'll bet the next 12 year old boy you see knows exactly who Tony Hawk is.

Branding based on research is frequently irrelevant, unimaginative and outdated. Time and again, the most enthusiastic survey respondents who swear that your product is the greatest won't spend a nickel to buy your product. If you have to survey your clients to know what they want, it's time to take the elevator from your ivory tower back to the ground floor.

"If I had asked people what they wanted, they would have said faster horses."

– Henry Ford

If you are looking to develop a great brand with a powerful position, don't look to your customer for answers or even approval. It is never the customer who comes up with the electric light bulb. It wasn't the coffee drinker who came up with duplicating the Milan coffee bar experience in the U.S. Not even the original owner of Starbucks, who was standing right in the middle of the goldmine, could understand the brand's scope. Genius level ideas don't come from the suggestion box (however the principle of the suggestion box is valid in another context). Great branding concepts come from obsessed, but in-touch business people deciding to brilliantly elevate their customer's experience … without permission, without surveys.

standing right in the middle of the goldmine

Brand Discipline

Whatever you do, your business soon earns a brand in your client's head. You can be the stumbling, bumbling never-delivers-on-time company. And you don't care one feather about branding. This is obviously the fast lane to business oblivion. But let's take this "bumbling, never-delivers-on-time company" and add a Branding Promise: "Crafting the world's finest acoustic, steel guitars." Suddenly you have used a Branding Promise to radically adjust your customer's expectations. Now we forgive you for slow delivery, faulty paperwork and even your arrogant attitude.

It's important that once you have a Branding Promise you exercise "brand discipline." This means that you don't confuse your staff with the "Branding Promise" of the month. You work hard to fulfill the promise of your brand. No one expects a Big Mac to be a work of gourmet art but they do expect it to be prepared in the time it takes to go through a drive-through. In 1955, McDonald's® founder Ray Kroc opened the first McDonald's® based on Dick and Mac McDonald's concept of a "Speedee Service System." This system was inspired by Henry Ford's assembly line used to produce Model T's. McDonald's® has changed over the years. Campaigns and slogans have come and gone. But the international food giant has been obsessive in its allegiance to this Branding Promise of a *speedee* food service system, the "True North" not only of their branding but also of their full worldwide range of operations even today.

Without a Branding Promise, you wearily try to meet a vast array of customer expectations and inevitably come up short. We call this the "Angel Complex." This psychological disease is usually accompanied by the desire to be all things to all customers. With a Branding Promise, you become intense, focused and suddenly … you are a business genius. An effective brand continually improves all aspects of a business, not just the sales and outreach.

> **Sometimes Branding just comes down to taking a real stand.**

People often ask, "So what will happen if I don't work on my company's branding?" The answer of course is, "Nothing." Exactly

nothing will happen. Branding is about taking a real stand … finding your working magic, seizing opportunity, and then going on a roll.

The following is a scene, known as "One Song" from the movie *Walk the Line* in which the main character, Johnny Cash, has 23 seconds – the chance of a lifetime – to communicate his brand and launch his career:

(Scene opens with Johnny Cash [Joaquin Phoenix] with his band in the legendary Sun Records studio, auditioning for Sam Phillips [Dallas Roberts], the genius who discovered Elvis, BB King, and Carl Perkins among many others. They are playing an old time gospel tune.)

the chance of a lifetime

Sam Phillips:	Hold on, hold on, I hate to interrupt. But you guys got something else? I'm sorry, I don't record material that doesn't sell Mr. Cash, and songs like that don't sell.
Johnny Cash:	Is it the music or the way I sing it?
Phillips:	Both.
Cash:	What's wrong with the way I sing it.
Phillips:	I don't believe ya.
Band Member:	Let's get out of here JR (Cash's nickname).

Cash: No, I want to understand. I mean, we come down here and play for a minute and he tells me I can't sing and I don't believe in God.

Phillips: (Impatiently) You know exactly what I'm tellin' you. We already heard that old gospel tune a hundred times just the like that, just like how you sang it.

Cash: You didn't let us bring it home.

Phillips: Bring it home? Alright let's bring it home. (Phillips leans forward with quiet intensity.)

If you was hit by a truck and you were lying out in that gutter dying, and you had time to **sing one song**, one song that people would remember before you're dirt, one song that would let God know what you felt about your time here on earth, one song that would sum you up – you're telling me that's the song you'd sing? That same tune we hear on the radio all day?

Or, would you sing something different? Something real?

believing in yourself

Something you felt, cause I'm telling you right now that's the kind of song that people want to hear, that's the kind of song that truly saves people.

It ain't got nothing to do with believing in God, Mr. Cash, it has to do with believing in yourself.

Cash: Well, I got a couple of songs I wrote in the Air Force, you got anything against the Air Force?

Phillips: (Shrugs his shoulders) No.

Cash: Well I do.

Johnny Cash then calls out the key to his band (later known as the Tennessee Three) who had never played the tune before. The song he sings is "Folsom Prison Blues." Phillips signed Cash to a recording contract on the spot and Cash began recording that day.

Cash turned out to be a stronger brand than Phillips ever imagined. His "Apathy Killers" were his deep, distinctive voice; the "freight train" sound of his Tennessee Three backing band; and his much publicized true passion for the inimitable June Carter; his rugged, outlaw image reinforced by his dark clothing, which earned him the nickname "The Man in Black." The Grammy Award-Winning country singer sold over 90 million albums in his nearly 50-year career and

"Folsom Prison Blues" became a huge hit in 1968, even beating out the Beatles.

Sam Phillips, as demonstrated above, knew the value of branding and separating from the pack. He was the first person in the South to have an "open" music format on the radio, i.e. playing both white and black artists, making stars out of both. Later, he hired only women as disk jockeys for his "All Girl Radio" format – another first. Most authorities credit Sun Records with producing the first Rock n' Roll song "Rocket 88" in 1951. When Sun Records hit a cash flow crunch, Phillips sold his Elvis contract to RCA Records. Don't feel sorry for him though – he invested the money in another great brand – the "Holiday Inn" hotel chain.

How Branding Relates to Selling

Branding is often reduced to the brand name – the logo and the slogan. When owners say they need branding, they usually mean identity. But the proper business of branding pertains to a world of significant sales system plug-ins essential to make any company grow. The whole branding package is the backbone of the selling effort.

Let's return to our riddle-definition of branding.

Branding weighs nothing yet it is the most valuable substance in the world. It is the essential grease and glue of business.

The entire brand of Nike® can be summarized on one page

The entire brand of Nike® can be summarized on one page. Most of the essential intellectual property could fit on a single hard disk. As we have said, it weighs nothing because the Nike® brand lives in the heads of its customers. But this branding substance is far more valuable than platinum, gold, or uranium. That's because a brand not only has intrinsic value but also has dynamic value, in that a brand can continually earn you money, sometimes lots of it.

Branding is business "grease" because ideally it eliminates all friction between your company and the customer. It lubricates the entire selling process, point to point, causing the client to slide effortlessly towards your brand.

Conversely, branding is business glue because it bonds your business to a defined crowd. This glue is called loyalty which is becoming an extremely rare, almost vanishing substance in many areas. When all the glue is gone, you find yourself selling a commodity – this is a position where no one wants to be.

Seven Ways Branding Directly Plugs into Sales

The main task of successful marketing is the consistent, persistent repetition of your brand to your customers, prospects and staff. Marketing is a mnemonic (memory) game. That's why the traditional "by the book" marketing tools like mission statements, marketing research and marketing plans have limited effectiveness. People just don't understand them, remember them or care about them.

Genius Simple Branding™ supports high touch laser and low touch drip selling in seven ways:

1. **Branding Promise** – In seven words or less, everyone, from the chairman of the board to the mailroom person, knows what the company is promising to the client. Every person in the company can keep the sales message consistent.

2. **Branding Map™** – Again, everyone is on the same page. Ten salespeople do not have ten different interpretations about what the boss may or may not think – the entire brand is clear.

3. **Go-to-Market Strategy** – All support sales materials are on brand. The logo, business cards, action cards, brochures, website, e-marketing, social networking tools and PR are all outstanding, unique, branded and thematically art directed.

4. **Finger-on-the-Pulse** – Instead of waiting for surveys or research that is old before you can act upon the information, salespeople (all staff with customer contact) are encouraged to detect and share any market shifts or trends for immediate action. Salespeople's ideas are listened to and valued. Marketing and Sales are cooperative.

5. **Hard Working Website** – Web site is intuitive and easy to use. Sales support is complete with FAQs, further reference, support options, contact info, online shopping cart, resources, tools,

tutorials. Information is current and SEO helps people find the company and learn what it stands for.

6. **Intellectual Property** – Sales has the Apathy Killers, Monkeys Paw, Credibility Kickers, Salty Sound Bites, Training Programs, Customer Guides to attract and support their crowd.

7. **Crowd Cultivation** – Genius Simple Brand™ is completely shaped for the right crowd so they can self actualize with the brand, lubricating the entire sales process. The brand supports and inspires its crowd for return sales.

Brands Can Get Sick – Avoiding "Cloudy Syndrome"

Cloudy Syndrome is a crippling disease that plagues many brands. It's as common as a cold. The "Cloudy Syndrome" makes your company appear foggy, dim, wavering, even undependable to a significant group of people: your customers and prospects.

Here are the five main causes of Cloudy Syndrome:

No Cohesiveness – You don't have a crystal clear Branding Promise with a Branding Map™ to keep customers, prospects, employees and leadership on the same page. You have always sold in the trenches – your sales team consists of survivors of the sink-or-swim school of selling. Your business has survived, even grown through sheer entrepreneurial willpower, but no one really "gets" what you stand for. For you, Cloudy Syndrome has been a permanent disability.

Garbage Collection – It is easy to be complicated. You add layer upon layer of flash-in-the-pan marketing ideas or strategies based on anecdotal experiences. You succumb to every new marketing fad. You make off-brand choices. Over the years your marketing becomes big and sloppy. You neglect the hard work of keeping your brand Genius Simple. Now is the time that Cloudy Syndrome sets in.

Disconnects – Everyone inside and outside of your company is telling a different story. You allow your brand not to make sense to your real market on some or many levels. Your brand winds up being marketed to everyone and appealing to no one. You now have Cloudy Syndrome.

Hand-to-Hand Combat – You are in the "bloody water" as they say in the book *BlueOcean Strategies*. Competition is fierce and you decide to be macho and duke it out with your competition. You play benefits one-upmanship or worse, you engage in a price war. You used to stand up for your client's well being. Now you stand up against the competition. Cloudy Syndrome is at your door.

Brand Extension – You are making a profit and have more elbow room in your budget. Suddenly, like the ancient sirens calling Odysseus to the rocks, opportunities start singing your name. So you decide to <u>diversify</u>, stretching your brand over "related" products and services. Immediately you take your eye off the ball of your main brand. The new products turn out to be sinkholes sucking the life out of the original brand. The market is now officially confused, and your business has Cloudy Syndrome.

sink holes sucking the life out of the original brand

Branding Courage – The Antidote

The best medicine for Cloudy Syndrome is a healthy dose of Brand Courage. People ask us all the time, "What happens if we focus too much on one crowd? Isn't it better to make our brand fit everyone. Won't we lose a lot of business? Most people see the fallacy of their concerns before they finish speaking them.

> *"You don't build it for yourself. You know what the people want and you build it for them."*
>
> **– Walt Disney**

courage to
focus

Finding one crowd and shaping a brand they love – think Disneyland and how it feels to children – takes courage.

The future belongs to two types of companies: 1) the huge mega-brands that have the muscle to dominate their markets with price, and 2) the specialists that position themselves as the savvy, well-branded standouts, who have the courage to <u>focus</u> continually, supporting and inspiring their loyal crowds.

DISCOVERY

"In every crowd there is a silver lining."
– P.T. Barnum

Who is My Crowd?

All of business begins and ends with your crowd. You have to find your crowd because that's where your customers and prospects come from. What your crowd thinks of your business determines your success. Branding exists in the minds of your customer and prospect base. So you can't really own or control the greatest asset of your business. You can proactively promote and passively attract. Marketing then is a balance of finding your crowd and letting your crowd find you.

If the truth be told, even if you think you can sell ice to Eskimos, there are some Eskimos who will never buy from a salesperson, no matter how talented, even if they need your product! Passive magnetic sales and referrals are necessary if you ever hope to reach this part of your crowd.

what keeps your customers up at night

You can start with a problem that needs solving, a need that must be met or a desire that requires fulfillment. Roll up your sleeves and tackle a big problem. The people for whom you solve that problem are your crowd. The odd discovery for us over the years is that most businesses start with a crowd. The founder is perhaps a member of a crowd who sold another member of the crowd something and knows in his heart he can do it again. For this entrepreneur, who is more common than you think, the solution or benefit comes later.

Once you identify your crowd, join them. Read the magazines they read, go to their events, make contact, and stay in touch. This is what we call "finger-on-the-pulse" marketing. Find out what keeps your customers up at night. Understand what they can't do without. Don't be like United Airlines® and spend thousands on research to find out what your customers want – by the time you read the report, the data is irrelevant. Be like JetBlue's® Dave Neelman, who keeps in direct contact with his crowd by flying on his own planes weekly, hanging around the ticket counter, working in the baggage area and even serving customers as a flight attendant. Be like Tony Hawk. As we said, there's not a 12-year-old in the United States who doesn't know his name. The skateboard park in his yard and his nationwide tours assure Tony that he will not miss a beat. If there is a shift in his market, Tony will know way before any research firm.

Just watch. Remember, they are your crowd if they say they are your crowd. Jeep® noticed an increase in women interested in their rugged

4-wheel vehicles. The Jeep® Grand Cherokee and Jeep® Liberty with a few comfort concessions opened a whole new market.

Respect your crowd. Your crowd is now interactive. If you cheat on your crowd and give them an unacceptable product on Monday (like Coca-Cola's® "New Coke" for instance), the whole crowd will blog you to oblivion by Tuesday morning.

> *"Markets don't want to talk to flacks and hucksters. They want to participate in conversations going on behind your business firewall."*
> **— Assorted Authors,** *"The Clue Train Manifesto, The End of Business as Usual"*

Your mission statement then, if you must have one, is the same for every company: Support and inspire your crowd!

Your customers are **YOUR CROWD.**

> *"Most people equate branding with the external image of a company, not the internal values, and to me that is where the greatest weakness is in companies."*
> *— **Mike Moser,** "United We Brand" (quote altered slightly)*

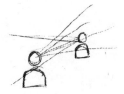

What are Core Values?

What does your business stand for? What are you passionate about delivering to your customer? "Core values you acquired, internal motivators you were born with," observed Ruby Mayeda of Dream Tank. "You must be true to both if you wish to find fulfillment and authenticity in your business." Your core values may not separate you from your competitors – they might be accepted practices.

The reason why core values are so important to establishing a Branding Promise is that you must have conviction in your branding. If you don't "buy in", how are your staff, customers and vendors going to feel the commitment?

Passion Has to Work on Planet Earth

It's wonderful to be passionate about what you do or produce but this passion must provide a relevant, undeniable benefit to your customer. You may be passionate about lead kites but will this fly with your crowd? The more appealing, unique, exclusive, and valuable this benefit is to your client the better. Remember to keep the ultimate benefit in mind. Concentrate on what you are really selling. You may be offering dance lessons, however what you are really selling is recreation and romance. When developing your relevant benefits, place yourself in your customer's shoes. Also, try to look at your business offerings as an industry "newbie" or a prospective customer might. This can be especially difficult because your business is probably second nature to you now.

Another aspect of relevance which is very important to consider is … are you fighting the right battle on the right battlefield? Here's an example: Do PDAs presently have to fight the battle to prove that they are a useful organizing tool, more effective than say … a Daytimer®?

The answer is probably no. That battle has long since come and gone. PDAs have achieved commodity status and now are fighting the price/features battle; they are morphing into cell phones, deploying Blue Tooth technology and drawing up other battlegrounds for the future.

When it comes to benefits, don't even try to make the obvious exciting.

The Sales Matrix – Do the Math

We've talked about concepts but the numbers always come up. You need to assess the number of leads you get per month compared to how many you need. You also need to know how many customers are in your database right now and do you have their physical addresses and e-mail addresses? This is important if you want to figure out the "critical mass" of clients, prospects and leads you need to grow your business. Benchmark and monitor web hits, e-blast "opens," auto responder hits, all in-bound sales calls and closes. The measure of a brand is sales.

> *"If you need to improve something, start by measuring it."*
> — ***Roswell et al.***

Benchmark and monitor

BRAINSTORMING AND PLUG-INS

Arriving at the Branding Promise

This is the part that causes Excedrin® headaches but also provides the greatest payoff. Developing your Branding Promise can take 15 minutes or 2 months. Here are the guidelines to defining your Branding Promise again in a slightly extended form:

1. **Seven Words or Less** – Should not be a sentence. Every word counts. One word is fine.

2. **Start With "You Get ..." No Matter What** – Must distill your firm's values, greatest benefit and sellable idea into one unified phrase. It doesn't matter if your office building falls down, you will deliver on this promise to your customer.

3. **Internal for Company** – slogan is for outside (clients, prospects) – A Branding Promise is not a hard sell slogan. It's internal for leadership, staff and strategic partners and vendors.

4. **Eliminate the Obvious** – Suggest, do not explain – a Branding Promise is the big picture condensed. It is not a core competency.

5. **Something You Could Be Best at – Doesn't Have to Make Sense** – 80 percent of what Americans purchase has no basis in logic. Finding something you can be best at means you can be the frog that rules the pond.

6. **Double Meanings are Welcome** – Occasionally you are lucky and a phrase has two meanings relevant to your brand. Arrive at your Branding Promise with brainstorming (see Module 4). We frequently go to at least 30 ideas. Then we use the process of elimination to arrive at the Branding Promise.

7. **"Corporate-Speak" is Forbidden** – This is not a dry-as-toner mission statement.

8. **What do You Stand For?** – Connect your primary value (theme word) to value for the customer.

Positioning – Branding Without Bleeding

Most businesses start out simply being a vendor – a seller of goods and/or services. Their position in the market is nonexistent – they are hoping to gain membership in the club. Outworking the competition, surviving the angel complex disease, emphasizing sales, and having the right attitude gets 20% of businesses to the next level which is preferred vendor. This is where many businesses stop developing – engaged in permanent hand-to-hand combat with their competitors.

For "Blue Ocean" people this is known as the bloody waters. This stage represents the crossroads where a business either gets bogged down or goes on a roll.

Brand development is the only way to escape the bloody waters. You carve out a market segment and shape your brand to that crowd. You evolve into a "trusted advisor" with irresistible IP. You create a pond with you as the dominant frog. The fastest growing companies are the ones that are not scrapping it out in the bloody waters – they are the companies that rule the fastest growing ponds.

The Lindbergh Law

Why is being first and only important - who was the second person to fly over the Atlantic Ocean?

At the trusted advisor stage you are quitting "the vendor club" and establishing your own brand of club with loyal members.

rule the fastest growing ponds

To go on a roll, you must have developed a "first and only" position in the market. This position allows you to generate both freelance buzz ("customers, co-workers, relatives and friends) and alpha buzz (writen, bloggers, industry leaders, networkers).

Changing Your Company Name – Arghh!

"Maybe so" in the words of the wise Zen priest. The right name is incredibly hard to find. But the task is made significantly easier once you have established your Branding Promise.

Analyze your name to see if it captures (optimum) or at least points to your Branding Promise. Sometimes you find that the name was your sales problem all along. Or you might find that it's just in neutral and does no branding work but at least is not an obstacle. Many lackluster names can be fixed with a slogan. You will be spending a lot of effort, time and money over the course of a business life getting your name in front of prospects and customers.

We believe in hard working names and logos. It is important that your name or naming unit (with slogan and trademark in tow) tells who you are, what you do and points towards (not explains, not spells out) your Branding Promise. If your name has momentum or is beloved in your market space, only change it with great caution.

Force yourself to decide:

A) The name is fine.

B) The name needs changing.

> *"Branding overnight is impossible. So break down your branding into the smallest steps possible. Take one or two of those steps each day. After a year, your brand will astound you."*
>
> **– Roswell**

⟩10 Name Game Rules

Naming a company, product or service can be a slam dunk or an excruciating process. As a brand catalyst, I rarely see the middle ground here. In over half of our GS Branding Maps,™ the name becomes an issue. Once we figure out a Branding Promise – True North for the brand – it becomes obvious that the name needs an adjustment. In about 20 percent of the cases, a totally new name is needed.

1. **Use your Branding Promise to determine your brand name** – Your Branding Promise is True North for your marketing. It's where you "plant your flag" as a company. So your name must fall in line if your want to have a cohesive, congruent brand.

2. **Your handle must not exceed three syllables** – Out of **Inc. Magazine's Top 50 Fastest Growing Companies** – the average "handle" (what people really call your company) has 2.4 syllables. For example: Orbit Design™ is four syllables but most people just use our handle and say "get Orbit (two syllables) on the phone." Go beyond three syllables and your branding will be destroyed with an acronym.

2.4 syllables

3. **Avoid acronyms at all costs** – Again out of the Inc. Top 50, the only acronyms used are by holding companies or parent companies that go to market with a properly branded product. Acronyms are only acceptable in the high tech arena where all the good names are saved for playing Dungeons and Dragons. Acronyms are brand killers. SuperSoft Pillows becomes meaningless as SSP. SSP is fine but it will cost twice as much to market.

4. **Suggestive names rock** – Names that suggest your Branding Promise, a benefit, a core competency, or client pain (as in BugBusters) – in that order – are optimum.

5. **Feels and sounds good** – Names that are easy and fun to say, with just one or two crisp, crunchy syllables in the mouth are desirable. Sometimes if the name is enhanced with alliteration, rhyme or double meaning, the name becomes easier to say and remember.

6. **Memory is everything** – If a name has traction, and people say, "Well I won't be forgetting that name will I?" then you have a winner – sometimes even if there are negative connotations. Graphic names – ones that call up a visual image (Apple® or JetBlue® for instance) are effective.

7. **Fanciful names are fine** – The trademark office refers to names that don't suggest a benefit as "fanciful." The name of your musical group or interior design firm must be fanciful. In an effective logo there are three parts: the name, the core competency and the slogan. Of the three, the name can be the most fanciful. What does Yahoo, or Google or iPod really mean?

8. **Generic means you are lazy and will pay** – Give your company or product a generic name (as in General Builders or Rocky Mountain "fill in the blank") and you will be punished for your

negligence. You will have to pay upwards of four times as much to go to market. In any competitive situation you will lose.

9. **Simple is better** – Okay, the drug companies pay tens of thousands of dollars for "pieces parts" – simulated product names like Paxil, Zantac, and Prozac. Simulated names can work if the pieces parts are suggestive as in rule number 3. Easy to say, spell and sell endears your name to clients. Difficult names in these days, are almost an insult to time-starved consumers.

10. **Do not let GoDaddy determine your name** – Web address availability should not determine your trade name. Only 1 percent of surfers find you by typing in your name. They will use a search engine and if your name is Lucky Joe's Restaurant and you come up www.xrwmzrs.com in Google, they will simply click, go to your site, and then add you to "favorites." Instead of GoDaddy, the U.S. Office of Patents and Trademarks database (www.uspto.gov) and the advice of a good lawyer are better guides in finalizing a name.

Of course, all rules are made to be broken and in the name game this is especially true. Many people get the disease Paralysis by Analysis in this area and that's fine. As you get feedback though, every name will have its detractors. So leadership should make a strategic decision based on positives for the company's brand. If there is anything special about your company: a program, process, philosophy, service, formula ect. be sure to name it.

"You name it...you own it!""

– Roswell

> Acronyms are Brand Killers

Acronyms are strangely popular in four industries:

> **Financial** – Every business stock has a symbol which is an acronym.

> **Medical** – Acronym is a second language you have to speak fluently.

> **Construction** – Construction people seem to lack the naming chromosome.

> **IT** – Let's face it. In the IT world acronyms have become a disease.

a group of letters says nothing

The problem with acronyms in a business or trade name is that they kill your branding. You have an opportunity in a trade name to say something memorable or meaningful about your business and a group of letters says nothing.

Why do people resort to acronyms?

There are three reasons:

1. **Acronyms are a shortcut for even worse brand killers** – The generic, painfully boring name. For instance, International Business Machines is IBM®, General Motors is GM®, General Electric is GE®.

2. **People hate names that exceed three syllables.** What they actually call you – your handle – is always subject to reduction. If you don't have a good handle and you name your business something like "Executive Headhunting International," you will inevitably be called EHI – and will have lost any chance at a meaningful, memorable brand.

3. **If you become the "800 Pound Gorilla" in your vertical, everyone will attempt to reduce your name to an acronym.** In politics, when John F. Kennedy, Lyndon Johnson, or George Bush become president the public lexicon reduces them to JFK, LBJ and W. In professional football there is no relevant competition so the 800 Pound Gorilla by default is the NFL (No Fun League). If you are the Gorilla who cannot be ignored, your name will be remembered no matter how bad it is.

So what if the name is hard to remember?

Branding, marketing and selling are purely a memory game. On average, any marketing initiative gets an immediate 1 percent response – in **the remaining 99 percent you may have more customers but they have to remember to buy from you.** If people don't remember you, the game becomes that much more expensive in time and energy. When four out of five new businesses fail within one year there is little room for error and a memorable, meaningful brand name can make a huge difference.

But What About IBM®? They Didn't do so Badly.

The name IBM® came into being in 1924. In that year there were less than 1,000 trade name applications. This year there will be upwards of 350,000. Currently there are a mind boggling 35 million domain names reserved. (No wonder we search for something like "Blue Zebra Umbrellas" and it's taken.) So IBM® flourished in a relatively tiny universe of trade names – nothing like what you and I face today.

Acronym fans please note that IBM® has a colorful, two syllable nickname "Big Blue" directly connected to their branding. Companies described as "All Blue" were loyal Big Blue customers. Their blue logo, patented shade of blue, signature blue business suits and blue mainframe computers more than managed to overcome the acronym handicap.

So having an acronym for a business name invites failure?

No, but why take the chance. Let's flip it and look at the 100 fastest growing businesses in the United States. You will find that 92 percent of the business names are not acronyms. And if we eliminate the four notoriously acronym-happy industries – financial, medical, IT and construction – there are **no fast growing companies** using an acronym name.

mind boggling 35 million domain names reserved

The Clever Slogan – Is It?

First, all company names, especially for small and medium sized businesses, need the help of a slogan. The slogan is your opportunity to memorably suggest your genius…magic…secret sauce…the night and day difference that makes your firm unique.   One way to look at slogans is that they exist halfway between a Branding Promise and an advertising headline. Good slogans have a bit of swagger. They are brief and leading but explain nothing. They salt the prospect's interest just like a headline but of course unlike a headline a slogan must click without a visual image. Avoid meaningless general concepts like "high quality," "low cost" – these are commodity-oriented words defining a space where "low bid" rules – a place where you don't want to be.

Two Tie-Ins for Your Slogan

First, take a look at your Branding Promise. Can it double as your slogan, as is? Your slogan must point to the True North of your Branding Promise so at the very least there are some key words you may be able to borrow. Or your slogan may complete or complement your Branding Promise. Nike's® successful Branding Promise of "Total commitment to one thing" is complemented by their super successful slogan, "Just do it." In other words, if you are totally dedicated to excellence, don't whine and complain, just go ahead and do it.

The other slogan generator is your Apathy Killer. Our firm Orbit Design™ uses this strategy, as Genius Simple Branding™ is both our Apathy Killer separating us from other design firms and our slogan.

Branding Promises and Slogans – Examples

Now that you've gone through the work on your own, below are examples from real life companies both large and small. You weren't given these right away to make sure the copycat factor helps your creativity along instead of heading off your initial ideas.

Company

Coca-Cola®   Promise: Delicious and Refreshing (1888)
Frank Robinson also designed the
logo (1904)

Today: To benefit and refresh everyone
it touches

Slogan: It's the Real Thing

Dell®   Promise: Accountability to each and
every customer

Slogan: Easy as Dell

GE®

Promise: Innovative ideas for the world's toughest electrical problems

Slogan: We bring good things to life

McDonald's®

Promise: The Speedee Service System (Modeled after Henry Ford's assembly line concept). Also, "Treat every customer with respect" (including children)

Slogan: I'm lovin' it

Intel®

Promise: Building block supplier to the internet

Slogan: Intel inside

Disney®

Promise: Providing quality entertainment and a world of magic for the entire family

Slogan: Welcome to the Magic – Imagineering

BMW®

Promise: Sheer driving pleasure

Slogan: The joy of driving

Nike®   Promise: Total commitment to one thing

                   Slogan: Just do it

Orbit Design™ Promise: The hum of genius

                   Slogan: Genius Simple Branding™

BSI 2000   Promise: When security matters most

                   Slogan: (same)

Blue Dot Solutions® Promise: Mobile computing made easy

                   Slogan: Intuitive mobile computing

Branding Icons

Branding icons make marketing come alive. They can be people, places, or things. They can be anything a person can sense: image, smell, taste, touch, sound. The only requirement is that they represent, dramatize and point to your Branding Promise. Branding icons are essential for getting your brand through that 23 second attention span window in your customer's head and staying there. People are the opposite of computers. We process images much more quickly than words, which our brains need to interpret first. So images (or all

getting your brand through that 23 second attention-span window

sensory data) are invaluable in gaining the attention of your best prospects and customers. Words have to be translated by our brains and can have greater staying power. The issue is not which is better – but how to get words and images working together for a synergistic sales effect.

Since the beginning of time, the most successful selling has been based on three types of images. First, oddly enough, are images of human beings – sometimes attractive ones called models, performers or athletes and other times ordinary people or "raving fans." Second, are animals, which have phenomenal marketing power. And third are toys in the broadest sense. The term in this context would include a BMW for instance.

Then there are the functional icons. First is the logo which essentially is a symbol designed to serve as an icon. Second, your product, or a "productized" version of your service is usually an essential icon. Third is the dominant color evoked by your branding. You should have input on the dominant color but experience proves that complementary colors should be chosen by designers who have been trained in color theory. And last is the invisible icon: context or place – where do your icons live?

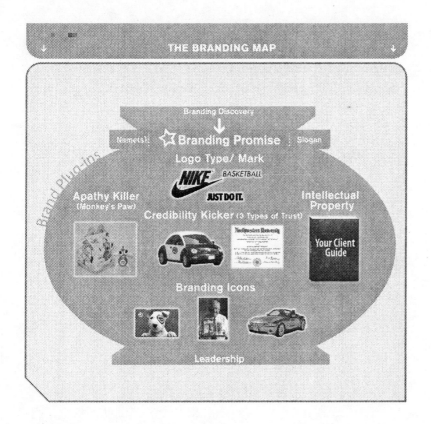

> Branding Icons and Your Designer

It is crucial that you talk over branding icons with your designer. You know your crowd the best. You understand what images are tried and true, edgy, tired, cliché, exciting and innovative. Developing branding icons that are pre-approved by you helps the designer stay on track to develop marketing tools that have the right look and feel for the job they must accomplish. Branding icons must be connected with your Branding Promise. However, if a branding icon logically connects to the Branding Promise and still doesn't feel right or seems out of sync, then your intuitive sense is trying to tell you not to use it. That is fine.

> **Branding Icon Examples**

Coca-Cola®	Red and white wave logo, Santa Claus, Polar Bears
	Color: Red
McDonald's®	Golden arches, Ronald McDonald, play structures
Nike®	Nike® swoosh logo, Air, Tiger Woods, John McEnroe, Michael Jordan
Mrs. Fields® Cookies	The smell of freshly baked cookies wafting through the mall.
	Color: Red
Harley Davidson®	Harley has actually trademarked the characteristic guttural sound made by their motorcycles. Their logo is everywhere.
	Colors: Black and orange

smell of freshly baked cookies

Velcro®	The unmistakable feel and sound of Velcro
Disney®	Mouse ears, Tinker Bell, Magic Castle Logo, all the Disney characters.
	Context: Magic Kingdom
Baskin Robbins®	31 Flavors. Context: Confectionary.
	Color: White
Godiva Chocolates®	Uniquely shaped candy boxes.
	Color: Gold
Orbit Design™	Space monkey logo, aliens and robots
	Color: Orange
	Context: Space

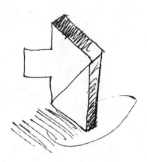

⸝ Branding Provides Congruency

You now have the foundation for an effective marketing system. Having a True North for all of your branding efforts will save you money, time and effort. Your messaging will stay consistent and congruent. You will be on the same page as your employees, vendors, board of directors and most important, your best prospects and customers.

"During recessions, people don't stop buying, they shift their buying."

— Roswell

Clydesdales and trusty Dalmatians

› Lessons from the Super Bowl

Again Animals Dominate 36 to 16 Over Human Superstars

What's in a branding icon? When companies are betting $3 million on 30 seconds of Super Bowl exposure (in the midst of economic disaster the price went up from $2.7 million last year), we branders take notes. Here are the final results of my informal, completely unscientific annual survey:

Again animals dominate. There were 36 animals (up from 32 last year) that starred in the 99 commercials recorded. They ranged from a ladybug to Clydesdales. If dinosaurs, bugs (hundreds), monsters (armies), and yes, five commercials featuring aliens are counted as animals, then the score becomes astronomically lopsided.

All of the top three winning commercials this year were produced by the planet's largest beer manufacturer – Budweiser®. Their perennial icons are some combination of Clydesdales and trusty Dalmatians. Last year, the number one commercial featured Hank, who enacted a Rocky-like climb to be the top Budweiser® Clydesdale with his faithful Dalmatian coach. This dog and pony show was unbeatable as they high-fived or rather high-hoofed/pawed each other in the final frame. This year Budweiser®

ads "Fetch," "Horselove" and "Clydesdale Ancestry" took 1, 2 and 3 respectively.

In Genius Simple Branding,™ we recognize Animals (even scary animals, monsters and aliens), People (stars or fun people) and Toys as the most effective branding icons. There is probably some complex, neuro-psychological, collective unconscious reason for this but the common denominator is probably fun – i.e. when faced with fun or no fun associated with a product or service, customers inevitably pick fun.

Often small business people feel that animals, people or toys would be silly in representing, in any way, their very serious product or service. Not only is their offering serious, but it requires lots of explanation, charts, diagrams, abstract symbols, etc. This attitude can lead to boring, ineffective marketing and disappointing results. Remember that branding is associative. Very simply, people love animals, people and toys and this love can rub off on you and your brand.

The Super Bowl threw many people at us – mainly athletes but Alec Baldwin and Jack Black were tossed in. Hall of Famer John Elway zoomed in on the Heroes "Football Game" commercial (voted 4th best). And the toys, with the exception of Mr. Potato Head were expensive – mainly cars – with a silent Jay Leno cruising in his classic Cobra taking best of class even over the main sponsor's

customers inevitably pick fun

"Hyundai as in Sunday." And the game? The people (Steelers) beat out the animals (Cardinals).

The Apathy Killer: Wow ... That's that Company that ...

Now we need to find the "triple that." You are comfortable with your Branding Promise. You are in the soft liquid center where it's safe and warm ... the boring middle perhaps. Now we have to take your Branding Promise to an extreme where it's cold, dark and unexplored. We have to go beyond the icon and discover the buzz, the epiphany maker, the contagious virus, the theme, attention getter, the Apathy Killer. We must go overboard to dramatize our Branding Promise.

If you are a world class company, going to extremes can be expensive. For instance let's revisit the Coca-Cola® company. "Idea to improve our brand: Let's build an entertainment center celebrating our product and let our crowd come and guzzle our soda out of a huge fountain to an outrageous degree. Let's make it three stories and fill it with 1,200 Coke artifacts, interactive displays and a huge fountain of Coke® products. We will even charge them $8 a head to get in. If there are not ten diabetic fits a day, then we are not doing our job." The buzz is "The World of Coke®," that's that crazy place where everything is Coke.

discover the buzz

Or your Apathy Killer can cost nothing, like Trail Dust Steak House. Idea to improve our brand: We've got an inexpensive steak house where families can relax and dress informally. It's a tough market because even a national chain of inexpensive steak houses failed in this city. Our Branding Promise is "great steaks in a relaxed atmosphere." We don't want anyone wearing a suit in our restaurant. In fact, anyone caught walking in the door wearing a stuffy old tie – well we'll … cut it off and … hang it on the wall. People buzz, "That's that restaurant that cuts your tie off and hangs it on the wall." Children insist on going to the Trail Dust Steak House at least once a year wearing a couple of their Dad's old ties, just so they can be cut off and mounted on the wall.

Or your Apathy Killer can simply be an offer that your crowd just can't refuse because it is amazing, free ok an incredible deal, or solves a problem they have always had.

An Apathy Killer is really effective when it uses a visual or something tied to the senses that directly connects with your Branding Promise. The Apathy Killer is a real world embodiment of your branding. Your business can have several Apathy Killers.

› Three Essential Building Blocks of Apathy Killers

> *"Vision is the art of seeing things invisible to others."*
> **–Jonathan Swift**

In the world of branding and sales, Apathy Killers must work overtime. No other marketing tool is quite as powerful, or as often neglected as a well thought out Apathy Killer; particularly among

"curiously strong mints"

small businesses eager to be a "member of the industry club" with a penchant for "me too" selling strategies.

As companies continue attempting to top one another with the most clever or visually stimulating mass market advertising on TV, Radio and in magazines, small businesses must keep in mind that this is a "low touch drip" sales strategy meant to keep advertisers top of mind. The response rate is so low that media tactics are wholly irrelevant to small business.

Small businesses must maximize their bang for the buck. A strong Apathy Killer must have a solid…

> **Hook** – An effective Apathy Killer must have a hook, similar to a Top 40 song. It should not only draw attention, it should also stick in the consumer's mind long after they first see or hear about it.

> **Connection** – An Apathy Killer cannot be effective without an explicit connection to your product or your company's Branding Promise. The Apathy Killer should relate directly to your marketing objectives, and enhance the brand image.

> **Buzz** – A truly great Apathy Killer not only draws customers in, it creates a buzz of excitement and dialogue among your crowd.

> **Apathy Killer Example**

Altoids® are the perfect example of how an effective Apathy Killer can make a product. Originally marketed as a stomach calmative to relieve intestinal discomfort, these "curiously strong mints" have reached almost iconic status in the United States thanks in large part to their distinctive tin can packaging. This packaging stands in stark contrast to the cheap, minimal foil and paper wrapping of competing products. From a functional standpoint, it provides no added value and is an unnecessary expense. Yet Altoids have continued to gain market share in the highly competitive mint sector, commanding a price premium of up to 400 percent.

> **Hook** – Altoids tins have a strong hook. Though not at all innovative or groundbreaking, their distinctive size and look set them apart from the efficient, functional packaging of other mints. Once a consumer sees this package in a supermarket checkout lane or in the hands of another consumer, they are unlikely to forget it: "That's that mint that comes in the little tin box."

> **Connection** – Altoids tins have a strong connection to the core branding of the product. They are a throwback to a time when products were less commercialized and of higher quality. These distinctive tins maintain Altoids'® status as a potent alternative to candy-like mainstream mints such as Certs® or Breath Savers®.

> **Buzz** – Altoids® tins have created a buzz among current and potential members of their crowd. Google "Altoids tins" and you will see a host of blogs and forums on creative uses for old Altoids tins. These tins are much more than just product packaging. Loyal

Altoids customers are using old tins to make iPod battery packs, cheese graters and even mini speakers.

In the right context, something as simple as a tin can drive more sales than you imagined possible. Carefully consider the hook, the connection and the buzz-worthiness of an Apathy Killer to dramatize your Branding Promise and separate your company from the pack.

> The All Time Apathy Killer Champion

McDonald's® is the all time champ at Apathy Killers. You are traveling and you can stop at either a gas station or a McDonald's.® You know that McDonald's® has consistently clean, warm interior restrooms for which you do not have to get a key (Apathy Killer 1). So you stop. You get out and your kids want the Happy Meal – one of the greatest Apathy Killers of all time (AK2). You decide to have an inexpensive combo meal featuring the Big Mac® (AK3) which comes with fries in under three minutes (McDonald's® original (AK4) "the Speedee Service System" the origin of the term "fast food"). After eating, the kids blast off to the interior playscape (AK5) and you get to sit down with your significant other and have a cup of coffee. That playscape was really built for you. Ronald McDonald (AK6) comes along to the delight of the kids. You gaze out at the famous Golden Arches (AK7) and see the sign for five billion hamburgers sold (AK8), and realize that by eating that burger (not the best in your neighborhood or any neighborhood really), you are part of something big.

That playscape was really built for you

The Apathy Killer is the catalyst for your advertising. It gives your copywriter the opportunity to develop a really "salty" headline that makes your customer thirst for more. It gives your designer a source that can be tapped for imagery. Your Apathy Killer should be a gold mine for creative ideas.

If you have a salty headline and tie it to a great visual, then you have a memorable selling concept. And what is selling but making your product or service memorable? Selling is a mnemonic game! In the war against "I don't care," the Apathy Killer is your magic wand.

Here are some "triple that's" or Apathy Killers that you might recognize:

That's that company that puts the "air" in your shoes.

That's that company that has the talking Chihuahua.

That's that company with the drinking polar bears.

That's that restaurant that was founded by Dave Thomas.

That's that company that lets you have fast food "your way."

That's that company that puts a prize inside the box with the caramel corn.

That's that company that has the mouse logo and the Magic Kingdom.

That's that company that has waiters on retro roller skates.

prize inside the box

That's that company that has the cars shaped like hot dogs.

That's that company that has the waiters that are rude to you on purpose.

That's that doctor who appears on the radio and promotes a heart healthy diet.

That's that company with the largest building in America.

That's that company that sells the water purifier with a light to tell you the filter needs to be changed.

That's that company that has a universal graphics file format that you can read using their free software.

That's that company that stays open all night to make copies.

That's that company that has the talking gecko.

That's that company that donates 5 percent of its proceeds to preserve the rain forest.

That's that company that sells a teenage girl doll that has a car and boyfriends.

That's that company that has auctions online.

That's that design firm with the aliens and creates Branding Maps.®

Here are two totally impartial Apathy Killers that will never work:

> > The post office delivers packages – but how about delivering packages overnight anywhere in the United States? Of course this would not only be impossible to do, but also the cost would be prohibitive.

> > You can get coffee **free** at the local gas station or nearly any waiting room – but how about selling premium coffee at a Milan-styled espresso bar and maybe jack the prices upwards of $3.50 a cup. Of course, people would never pay $3.50 and up for something they brew every morning in their kitchen for a few pennies.

It can be the prize inside, an added benefit, a secret ingredient, a frequent user card, a tagalong gift or an authentic bonus. Wrigley gum was originally just a tagalong gift attached to a bar of soap – an Apathy Killer that grew into a top selling product.

Take your Branding Promise to an extreme and make your point to the world about your product or service even if you have to radically change your product or service. A Branding Promise can make your company infinitely better.

The Credibility Kicker

We have gotten their attention. We have ventured out of our comfort zone to prove a point to our customer. We have pointed toward our Branding Promise and offered our core benefit. But the whole sales situation still feels like a "leap" to your prospect. So you have fence sitters. This is where the "Credibility Kicker" comes into play. The Credibility Kicker is an advertising or point of purchase concept that "kicks" the customer over to your side by winning trust.

> *"A monetary goal is like cotton candy — looks great and tastes sweet. But the vision and the people provide the lasting satisfaction."*
>
> *– Roswell*

simply brings people back to their comfort zone

❯ Are You Trustworthy?: The Four Types of Customer Trust

In selling products and services, businesses must generate trust or the marketing game is over before it begins. Trust is defined as "a willingness to rely on an exchange partner in whom one has confidence." Trust is the foundation of any sales situation whether it be "low touch" on the web or "high touch" as in face to face selling.

Apathy Killers, as we have discussed, are sexy attention getters that highlight the Branding Promise of a company and typically stretch your customer's limits – in a good way. Then there is the antidote to the Apathy Killer – the Credibility Kicker, which simply brings people back to their comfort zone and saturates them with trust factors. When you are doing a "sell, sell, sell" marketing piece, you lean towards the Apathy Killer, When you are doing a "leave behind" marketing piece, you lean towards the Credibility Kicker. Actually both need trust to work, but each elicits a different type of trust.

In the "Three Types of Trust", a 2002 study (McKnight, Choudhury and Kacmar), three important types of customer trust were identified: ability, benevolence and integrity. To this group, our experience drives us to add a fourth: **enthusiasm**.

Why do marketer researchers bother to separate these types of trust? The reason is that if you break down trust, then you are better able to take real measures to build – or maybe repair – specific types of customer trust.

Ability – Can you do the job? Stress innovative capabilities or products (making competition obsolete). Show how your capabilities far exceed the customer's expectations. Practice what you preach – congruency adds to your trust equity. If you are selling a sleek, hi-tech product make sure your marketing materials are sleek and hi-tech. Conversely, if you are selling inexpensive, environmentally friendly products, print on recycled paper. "The medium is the message" was coined by the sage Marshall McLuhan. This is the area where your Apathy Killer shines. You are highlighting your particular area of competence.

Integrity – Do you meet third party standards in your field? This is the area where academic credentials, endorsements, respected membership organizations and publishing generate credibility.

Benevolence – Are you only in it for the money? Inject genuine support and concern into your marketing and make money a secondary issue. For example, if you manage investments, lead with education and information – leave discussions of net worth for later. Customers value authenticity. If everything you do "smells of sell", then your trust level goes down. Recent market research indicates that the old sales truism "service with a smile" is untrue. Prospects buy more when they feel the salesperson is concerned, genuine and informed. They mistrust smiles, glad handing and the overly friendly approach. Price is an indicator of benevolence – do your customers feel gouged?

In my experience this survey left out the fourth and most important trust factor:

enable the customer to see their own greatness

Enthusiasm – Are you excited about doing the job or providing the product? This is the most under-rated factor in trust and I feel the one that is of utmost importance in winning any job from lawn care to designing airports. People can forgive any of the other trust factors if your enthusiasm for their project is real and plainly visible. You must be genuinely excited and if you can take the next step and successfully enable the customer to see their own greatness reflected in the proposed project – the job is yours.

⟩ Marketing Pieces and Trust

Even the wildest or most extreme ad or direct mail piece (sell, sell, sell) must have trust signals if it is to be successful. Of course any decent Apathy Killer, with its over-emphasis on the firm's Branding Promise, is going to signal trust in ability. However, complete passion for a product or service also gives a strong benevolence signal – i.e. would we be this fanatical if we were only concerned about money?

The Credibility Kicker (the closer) is where customer integrity trust lives. From endorsements to credentials, the Credibility Kicker looks outside the company for integrity trust factors.

In some instances, the Apathy Killer and the Credibility Kicker are the same. Best Buy,® known for their low cost strategy, developed an extremely successful Apathy Killer/Credibility Kicker blend in the Geek Squad.® With its fleets of heavily branded VW® Beatles, many people would never shop Walmart® or Costco® for a computer, but Best Buy® – with the exact same low price strategy – is acceptable because "those Geek Squad® service people know what they are doing". I have said these very words myself realizing that some Best Buy® brander skillfully planted the thought in my head.

An effective brand carefully addresses each of the three types of customer trust.

Ultimately the brand itself becomes the Credibility Kicker. The saying "No one ever got fired for buying IBM"® is an example. Or the

attitude: "I will buy any product with the word SONY® on it – I don't even have to read the product reviews because I know that SONY® puts out good products. I will even pay a little extra if the brand name is on it." Or the famous "If you don't have Coke,® I'll just drink water."

The Credibility Kicker is invaluable for self-talk and word of mouth referrals. It makes consumers say to themselves, "Well if it doesn't work out, you can always … return it, use it for something else, revitalize it for free, use the bonus which is almost as good as the product, resell it, get the difference because it has a guaranteed low price." Some people want the Credibility Kicker more than the product. The Credibility Kicker guarantees the value and makes the customer feel safe in making the purchase. Hopefully you have won the emotional battle with your Apathy Killer so the Credibility Kicker gives customers a reason to rationalize buying your product.

Intellectual Property (IP) – Unlock Working Magic

I am always astounded by the fact that business owners spend tons of valuable time developing their intellectual property (IP) and keep it under wraps. It may be a process, a program, a guide, an invention, a curriculum, a secret ingredient, a song/jingle, a recipe, an image, a branding icon, a style … and they never give it a properly branded name. Even when the IP is an integral part of the business' sales strategy.

Be it suggestive or fanciful, when you name something you own it. Humans, except for building contractors and IT people have a genetic disposition to naming. Naming intellectual property enables you to brand and take it to market. In the information economy, intellectual property will gain an increasing amount of emphasis by businesses.

This IP treasure we unearth in the Branding Map™ discovery process is often a reservoir for much of the company's cumulative industry knowledge, and yet is often ignored or dismissed.

Intellectual property is the great separator, the ultimate Apathy Killer, for many contemporary businesses. As such, careful protection is required. There is an amazing amount of misinformation, misconception and mythology around copyright and trademark law.

> *"A good brand is that all important plus factor for your business that works silently, persistently, cumulatively every day to build your business. Like compounding interest it can yield exponential results."*
>
> **– Roswell**

> Protecting Your Brand – Part I: Copyright

Intellectual property (IP) is often the "magic" that sets you apart from the competition. It's one of your company's most important assets and something that must be protected from the increasing number of businesses willing to steal and copy your creative works.

We know you've got more pressing needs to worry about, but in a world where the transfer of information has become faster and easier, it's more important than ever to protect and defend your intellectual property.

We recommend that you take a few minutes and register your works through the United States Copyright Office. Here's a list of the types of works that can be registered (Note that the definitions of these works are very broad. To see explanations and examples of each type click on the links below):

> **Literary works** (example) including text based works and books, brochures, guides, catalogs, white papers, instructions, all marketing materials, etc.

> **Sound recordings** (example) including music CDs, workshops, speeches, etc.

> **Visual art works** (example) predominantly art and design works including original graphic work, images, diagrams, textile designs, sculpture, drawings, etc. Note: A contact sheet of multiple photographs can be registered as a group for one filing fee.

> **Serials/periodicals** (example) newspapers, magazines and other business publications like newsletters, e-blasts, etc.

> **Performing art works** (example) any theatrical or dance piece (if the choreography has been notated this may also be registered).

The whole process takes less than 30 minutes and costs $45 plus postage. An online registration form is scheduled to be available sometime this summer, but has yet to be released. (When it is released the forms will be changed so watch for the release). Until that time, to complete the copyright process, here are the steps that you must take:

1. Affix the word copyright and/or the symbol © to your work with the year and the name of the entity owning the copyright: (example) Copyright © 2007 John and Susan Smith

2. Go to http://www.copyright.gov/register/

3. Determine the type of work you want to register and click on the appropriate button.

4. Print and fill out the required form (this will be a .pdf file) make sure you print the form on one sheet, front and back head to head. Remember to sign the application.

5. Send the work, along with the completed form and a $45 check payable to the Register of Copyrights, to the US Copyright Office – the address is on the form.

6. That's it. You'll be notified when the process is complete.

Note that the process takes some time. All mail is sent to a screening site where it may be damaged when irradiated.

takes less than 30 minutes and costs $45

The common notion that a work is protected by copyright law the minute you create it is true – but extremely misleading. Why? Because if in the future you are trying to prove infringement, you will have no third party evidence to prove that you did indeed create the work yourself. The "poor man's copyright" – sending a work to yourself in a sealed envelope – ranks just slightly above inadequate as a means to protect your IP and is considered to be an "old wives tale by lawyers." **Registration with the Copyright Office is the only way to protect your full array of rights under present U.S. copyright laws.**

> *"Giving is the most effective sales strategy."*
> **— Dave Block,** *Make-it-Fly®*

⋗ Protecting Your Brand – Trademark

You now have a new company, product or service name and a logo. Is this my brand? What is a trademark and is it different than a trade name? Can you have more than one trademark? How do I protect a trademark? Do I need a lawyer?

First, a trade name and a trademark are often confused with a business' brand. Trademarks (or trade names) make up a subset of your overall business brand which includes images, processes and intellectual property that engages your target market, evoking certain mental stimuli in your clientele's mind. Powerful brands promote success and are often an organization's most valuable asset.

A trademark is the term used for a distinctive, unique mark or design that sets your business apart from your competition. It may or may not be registered in the US Patent and Trademark Office. If registered you are provided with national protection and have taken the first steps toward acquiring foreign protection. The scope of what a trademark is has few boundaries. If something is capable of uniquely indicating your business, it can be considered a trademark. This might include a word, graphic, logo, symbol, name, slogan, shapes, sounds, smells, moving images, taste, and texture. Nike® has registered the famous "swoosh" symbol. "IBM Blue®" and "Kodak Gold®" are colors that have been trademarked.

Our legal system has several protective measures for intellectual property: copyrights, trademarks and patents, which can occasionally overlap. For example, a graphic design of a logo will have a unique graphic quality, which may include your company's name and slogan. While the name can be protected as a trade name and the logo (or combination of name and logo) can be protected as a trademark, the design elements may also be copyrightable artwork.

In many states, a trade name is the name your company conducts business under and uses for commercial purposes. As such, it is the name that you should register with the Secretary of State's Office when you form your business entity – be it a DBA, an LLC or a C or S Corp. This sort of registration precludes others from using your

name in your state and it puts your name into several national databases used for research for federal trademark availability.

After registering with your state, the next step is to place a TM symbol next to any name, logo, symbol or image which you feel is indicative of your particular business. Using this symbol establishes minimal protection; only registration affords full, legal protection nationwide. Anyone who claims rights to a trademark may use the TM (trademark) designation to alert the public to the fact that the name or logo is being used as a trademark. It is not necessary to have a registration, or even a pending application, to use these designations. The claim may or may not be considered valid in a court of law.

"You can build a magnificent, cohesive brand, but if you fail to get the word out and neglect driving traffic to your branded website, even a great brand will die on the vine."

—Roswell

❯ Protecting Your Brand – The Registered Trademark

The registration symbol ® may only be used when the mark is registered in the United States Patent and Trademark Office (USPTO). It is improper to use the registration symbol at any point prior to registration. The USPTO's web address is www.uspto.gov. It is very user friendly and you can even look up current registered trademarks on your own. However, to register a trademark requires a careful decision on your part, with the advice of an intellectual property lawyer. Note: this is not the lawyer that did your will or divorce.

What is the difference between a trademark (™) and a registered trademark (®)? Both symbols allow you to claim the rights to your trademark and provide notice to third parties of the fact that you are using it as a trademark, but each has its pros and cons.

> A ™ next to your mark signifies your claim to ownership of a trademark that is not registered with the federal system. One can use this notice as soon as the trademark is put into action.

> > **Pros:** This is the fast free way to control the use of your IP. It is recognized by the United States judicial system as common law, and, to a certain extent, allows the owner to legally pursue the unauthorized infringement or use of this trademark.

> > **Cons:** The legal ramifications are usally limited to protecting the trademark only within the geographical area(s) where the mark is being used, or within which the mark is reasonably expected to be recognized. For example, if you use a trademark in Colorado and have registered your trade name with the Colorado Secretary of State's Office, you may be protected within the State of Colorado and perhaps in closely surrounding areas.

> The ® notice signifies that you have registered the mark with the USPTO, and legally cannot be used until you have received the certificate of registration from the USPTO.

each has its pros and cons

> **Pros:** This course provides a more substantial legal claim to ownership with exclusive rights of use. Registering your mark (in most cases) allows you to prevent unauthorized use in an exact or similar vertical through legal proceedings for trademark infringement. In specific instances, you can also prevent the use of your trademark in completely dissimilar products/services, depending on whether or not a consumer could be confused as to the identity of the goods and/or services. For example Microsoft Bakery would not pose as an infringement to Microsoft Software®, but Microsoft Televisions just might. For another example, you could not simply open a restaurant and call it McDonalds as customers have come to associate that name with a rather large group of hamburger joints.

> **Cons:** Registering a trademark federally can be a lengthy process, not to mention expensive. You also need to make sure you have something to protect and that would not be considered generic. A trademark can only be registered if it meets the requirements set forth by the USPTO and has distinctive characteristics.

> So how do you know which course of action works best for you?

Let's say you're a local business, with only a few clients in other parts of this country. While you offer something unique for your clients, you're not the only business of your kind. First, register your trade

name with your state's Secretary of State. Second, review your mark by doing your own research. Look at the search engine on the USPTO's website, go to various search engines on the internet and enter your proposed mark. If you find potential problems, you might want to entertain the idea of a new name or you might want to talk to a lawyer. Otherwise, you might spend time and money building your business only to receive a nasty cease and desist letter from another company using the same name!

Let's say your company name has geographical references, like "Denver Widgets," and your branded icons follow suit. Rather than worry about changing everything to meet registration requirements, keep your trademark focused on your brand. TM your trademarks.

Let's say your company, like many others, has multiple trademarks. We recommend that you consider registering the most valuable or unique one or two. Use careful consideration to determine what is most proprietary and specific to your business, and potentially the most likely to be ripped off. If you have a special or unique graphic that is what you'll need the most protection around. Many times you'll find that while your name, logo, and slogan are unique to your business, one or more may not be the most worthy of protecting. For example, let's say you manufacture genetically altered potatoes that cause one to lose weight. Not only is this a patent worthy discovery, but your packaging should be a registered trademark.

Or whatever it is that will set you apart when other companies start trying to pass off similar products.

If your business is international, it is better to be safe than sorry. Many other countries have the philosophy of "first to file" as opposed to "first to use." Countries such as China or the European Union do not recognize trademarking through use, and you could find yourself at a loss in a trademark dispute, not only in pursuing legal damages for infringement, but in losing the capacity to use your own trademark! Register your trademarks. You may find it worth every penny in avoiding process pains.

Keep in mind, to maintain the rights of ownership of your trademark, registered or not, requires continuous use in commerce as well as continued policing or enforcing your rights in the event of infringement. There is no hard and fast rule, but you normally have about five years of inactivity before you no longer retain ownership of that trademark.

Tip: Microsoft Word on the PC allows you to type just T for ™ or R for ® while holding down the Ctl and Alt keys. Those running MacOS can hold down the Option key and type 2 for ™ and r for ®.

Thank you to the law firm of Repelin & Rhoades LLC, specialists in Intellectual Property Law, for reviewing for accuracy this text on copyright and trademark protection.

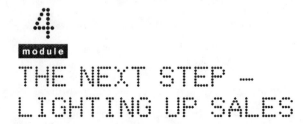

THE NEXT STEP —
LIGHTING UP SALES

"It is easier to sell to your worst enemy then to a confused customer."

– Roswell

The "Go-to-Market Strategy" – A simple, powerful tool for selling

At the completion of the Branding Map™ process, The question arises … what's next? Having witnessed the lack of concreteness in many marketing plans, the best plan of action is to create a "Go-to-Market Strategy," which is just that. An easily understood list of planned actions that brings your brand into the sales process. In the spirit of Genius Simple, the "Go-to-Market Strategy" takes the simple form of a checklist. Explanations are minimal but are included so the plan can be picked up at any point and continuted. The action plan is designed

24/7 perpetual sales engine

workable
to-do list

to give the fastest results while developing a 24/7 perpetual sales engine for your firm.

If complex strategic marketing plans sit on the shelf and collect dust, this is not because the concepts are without value. They are often just not "actionable" – in the same way writing a novel is not actionable. Writing an outline for a novel or writing an opening sentence is actionable. It is simply a matter of breaking down a large, forbidding project into do-able chunks.

How do you convert a brand into lasting change, into a vital multi-channel sales system for your company? One step at a time.

A Go-to-Market Strategy is stripped of all extraneous material and contains only required actions and products. If you have ever been exposed to a corporate strategic marketing plan, you know that they consist of heavily documented justifications including charts and graphs for adopting a particular strategy. The goal of many marketing (and business plans) is consensus on the part of investors, lenders or potential partners.

The purpose of a Go-to-Market Strategy is action. It takes careful thought on the front end. What are you keeping and what do you need to develop for your sales system? What initiatives need to happen? Can we break them down into doable tasks? Can some of the tasks be done concurrently? Who will do these tasks? Can we prioritize the whole list? And finally, can we set it to a reasonable budget and timeline?

This workable to-do list rquires that completed items be checked off as tasks are completed. We developed the idea of a Go-to-Market Strategy in response to customer requests for a sales process as simple and direct as the Branding Map™. This has worked so well that Orbit Design has created Fast Forward Passport - a password protected microsite where you can work on your Branding Map + Go-to-Maket Strategy online with complete online support.

Stick With Your Branding Promise

You now have your Branding Promise. At Orbit Design,™ we have placed the Orbit Branding Promise on every computer. The next thing you must do persistently, consistently and obsessively is to begin keeping your Branding Promise to your clients and prospects.

Likewise your marketing must be consistent, persistent and obsessively repetitive. Speaking of obsessive, let's look at Coke again. Reviewing the history of their advertising, it is centered on their branding to an almost scary degree. Here are some sample headlines from the history of Coke promotions since 1888: Coca-Cola® was founded by chemist John Pemberton in 1886. He described his creation as "delicious, exhilarating, refreshing and invigorating." He died in 1888 and handed over the company to Asa Candler, owner,

Frank Robinson
genius level
salesperson

who hired Frank Robinson, genius level marketer/sales, person, who designed the Coca-Cola® logo and the Branding Promise:

Delicious and Refreshing™

Be Really Refreshed™

Coke Refreshes You Best™

Delicious and Refreshing™

Deliver Refreshment™

Drink Coca-Cola®™

Drive Refreshed™

Go Refreshed™

Good to the Last Drop™

It's the Real Thing™

Real™

Real Refreshment™

Refresh Yourself™

Refreshment Right Out of the Bottle™

Shop Refreshed™

Sign of Good Tasting Refreshment™

The Cold Crisp Taste of Coke™

The Power That Refreshes™

The Sign of Good Taste™

The Taste That Refreshes™

Thirst Asks Nothing More™

Thirst Knows No Season™

Of the 34 "Themes for Coca-Cola® Advertising from 1888 to 1999" in the Library of Congress, 20 feature women, 12 feature men (one is Santa Claus whom many feel was shaped in our minds by the

Coca-Cola® Company), 3 featured animals (eagle, dog and most famously polar bears). Interestingly, Coke marketers are obsessive about persistent, consistent repetition. All 34 visual themes contain the Coca-Cola® logo and the product in one form or another. In 1888 Coca-Cola® was only available as a fountain drink but a glass of the product appears in all of the theme ads and in one there is a Coca-Cola® soda fountain.

> *"The great thing in the world is not so much where we stand as what direction we are moving."*
> **— Oliver Wendell Holmes**

> *"When selling: One ounce of 'support and inspire' equals a pound of 'sell'."*
> **— Andy Cleary,** *Genius Simple Design*

Ten Steps to a Genius Simple Outreach System

Your brand drives your sales. Your sales drive your company. That's why you contact your customer base regularly with branded low touch mailers/e-blasts, you create and follow up hot leads with high touch sales calls, you have an organized sales database of leads and current customers, and you are in consistent dialogue with all of your clients, ensuring that no potential sales fall through the cracks.

Or at least that's what you want to be doing. In the real world you are being pulled in a million different directions. You are constantly busy, but are you capitalizing on the potential that's out there? Without a

starting from scratch every time you make a sale

fully branded outreach system you are starting from scratch every time you make a sale. Here are ten steps to formulate your outreach system.

1. **Analyze** – How Do You Get Your Best Customers? Is there a pattern? If so, can you externalize it and get it down on paper. What is the sales process point by point? What parts of the process are replicable and repeatable?

2. **Brainstorm** – Explore both the outreach systems you have relied on in the past (improve them) and explore new ideas. Consider unorthodox methods. Make a Top 100 list of desired clients.

3. **Plan One Year Out** – Put together a sales calendar. Make high touch laser, networking, speaking, and organizational commitments. Schedule your Low Touch Drip sales efforts and commit time to them.

4. **Evaluate** – On an ongoing basis log in an evaluation of each sales activity. The most important part of your evaluations is determining what is replicable and can apply to your outreach system approach. Isolate the good, throw out all the fluff. Is that ad producing – is your search engine optimization (SEO) productive? Take the revised version of your process and make an outline from initial customer contact through closing the sale.

5. **Become a Part of Your Crowd** – Read what your customers read, join the groups they join, attend the events they attend. Customize your outreach system to fit them.

6. **Read Your Local Business Journal** – Find out who is doing what and is connected with whom. Identify individuals and groups who might fit your Top 100.

7. **Use Social Networking to Refine Your Laser Selling** – Is your networking more like selling by wandering around? Can social networking such as "Linked In" help you streamline your networking? You want to find people who need your services.

8. **Optimize Your Sales Materials** – Make sure your sales materials sell like you sell. Power Point presentations should be clear and compelling. Leave-behinds should echo your branding messages and evoke trust.

9. **Sales Training** – Have a professional or mentor look at your outreach system. You may be a seasoned veteran and still have a lot to learn – there is no shame in asking for help – Tiger Woods has six coaches.

10. **Seek Editorial** – Editorial costs time but not dollars and is ten times more credible than a display ad.

non-standard tools

Genius Simple Design

Genius Simple Branding has its expression in the design of sales tools. This is a whole separate topic. However, Orbit Design has become known for our non-standard tools from business cards to brochures to websites and feel that it is important to go into how this works and why. The focus here will be on the business card as the standard bearer for all sales materials and on your office or studio as an atypical area for branding to manifest itself.

❯ The Standard Run-of-the-Mill Business Card

I have only one question about the standard, run-of-the-mill business card – Why would you want one? Do you have a standard, run-of-the-mill business?

Branding, by definition, sets you apart from the crowd by making you memorable, distinctive and magical. To a company developing a vital brand, any standard run-of-the-mill sales piece is simply a waste of time and money.

Business cards are used in over 94 percent of successful business-to-business transactions. It is the hub of the "high touch laser marketing" that Orbit Design™ promotes. It's not only a great feeling when potential clients say "wow" when they get your card but you are immediately giving several positive impressions:

94% of successful business-to-business transactions

1. If you put this much into a card – you must put even more into your product or service.

2. You're probably the "alpha" or standout in your industry.

3. I will remember you because your card was memorable.

4. You are not afraid to be different – this makes my defenses go down.

5. I get you – I get your core capability (yawn) but I can feel your enthusiasm through your card. (wow). You are really committed to what you do.

6. You have given me a reason to go to your web.

7. Your card has buzz and is worth showing off to others.

sales morgues

Here is the #1 objection to "non-standard" business cards:

1. Your card doesn't fit into my plastic page slots, or my rolodex, or my wallet, or my...you name it. Your card sticks out.

My question is always – Do I really want to be in your page protector notebook slot or rolodex (do they still make these ugly contraptions?) and I definitely don't want to be in the wallet you sit on all day. The aforementioned are just places where you bury both me and my business card – they are sales morgues. I want a living business relationship, therefore my goal is to be in your:

❯ Outlook or whatever contact software you use

❯ In your PDA or your Blackberry®

❯ In your telephone speed dial list

❯ Out on your desk when you get back to the office

If I am not in or on one of these, we are probably not going to do business together.

Here are some quick tips for creating an "alpha" business card:

> **Never do the standard size – 2" x 3.5"** – God never decreed that business cards had to be 2 x 3.5. Actually I don't know who did. We have clients who can't wait to give out their cards.

> **Use professional design** – People can tell the homemade look a mile away.

> **Explore different materials** – especially if they are "suggestive" of your brand (an aluminum card if you make aluminum products)

> **Explore different shapes** – It's a definite "wow" and not as expensive as you might think. Folds can also create interest.

> **Use your auto-responder or your referral program (if appropriate)** – Drive prospects to your web.

> **Use both sides** – It's a simple matter of more room to "support and inspire" your prospect.

Don't keep business cards in a wallet you sit on or crunch. They will look like wilted lettuce. When networking, never drink or eat food. I have seen so many comical juggling acts and have been myself somewhat of a clown. Have a quick bite or sip beforehand if you must and take your networking time seriously. Do not keep your business cards in a holder – it seems pretentious and time consuming for the other person.

Orbit Design™ has become known for innovative business cards, sales materials, web sites, and e-marketing tools. That is the subject for our next book.

Branding Your Web

Look to your Branding Map to drive your web design. Apathy killers define your main navigation pathways. Your name, icons and autoresponder are all called out in the map. Always have your Elite Eight in mind as visitors. Your web should be a virtual Disneyland for the top one or two crowds and their alpha influencers. Finally your massaging is spelled out in your Branding Map. Web 2.0; "web without walls"; "don't make me think intuitive webs" are approaches that merit continued discussion (and are beyond the scope of this book) but driving your web with "core buzz" is one of your Branding Map's most important roles.

Branding Your Space

If you have ever visited the famous Apple® retail store on Fifth Avenue in New York, you may have realized that in a city that is entirely about vertical real estate value, this store is unthinkably flat. Approaching the store, you see just a glass cube about 30 feet high with a luminous Apple® logo suspended in the center. Obviously influenced by I.M. Pei's glass pyramids at the Louvre, the interior of

"Rescue Room" for their clients

the store is flooded with natural light from the surface cube. There are no windows. The rest of the store is entirely underground like a bunker and it just drips with the Apple® brand. Every product, big screen TV, salesperson, work and play stations, and signage integrate into a cohesive experience for Apple fanatics from 5 to 95 with a mantra of "think different."

Even devoted Windows® users thoroughly enjoy this pinnacle store that rivals the World of Coke® as a thoroughly iconic experience.

These days, customers feel there is a disconnect if you have a vital brand everywhere, but your office, showroom, brick and mortar store or even your production/manufacturing area is pure "vanilla." Yes, every space, even law and accounting offices are in for major changes. In fact, one of our legal clients, St. Bernard Bankruptcy,® recently hired an interior decorator to help develop a "Rescue Room" for their clients. This themed room will offer a calm atmosphere, refreshments and reassuring educational pieces for debt stressed clients.

Orbit's "Robot Room" is a toy dotted area with a comfortable sofa, lounge chairs and a wet bar with refreshments – not a conference table in sight. During long branding sessions, clients feel comfortable enough to kick off their shoes, curl up on the couch, and explore the toy robots, while pondering the future of their company.

your brand's separation from the "run-of-the-mill"

Do you need expensive modifications requiring an interior designer? Not necessarily. But to avoid looking off-message or unintentionally tacky – thorough brainstorming and careful implementation with someone whose taste you trust is necessary. You can err on the lighter side for a simple reason: when faced with boredom versus even the smallest attempt at fun, customers will choose and appreciate fun every time.

"designing by committee"

What does branding your space mean to your customer? There are three significant messages: First, you are demonstrating the authenticity of your brand – it permeates every corner of your company, right down to the factory floor, and is not just on the surface. Second, you are clearly stating your commitment to your customer's entire experience. And third, it underscores your brand's separation from the "run-of-the-mill" vanilla competition.

Brainstorming Model for Branding

The sole purpose of branding is to drive sales. In this book, the emphasis is on developing your brand so that it plugs directly into the sales process. The most effective brand by far, the Genius Simple Brand, is not easy and requires a lot of thinking and planning. Most of the brand aspects require brainstorming.

Now most people know how to brainstorm. As a creative agency we have tried many methods. And it is important to understand that creativity is often an individual activity. Once a brainstorm feels like you

are "designing by committee," it is probably time to stop and break out for individual attention to the problem. The brainstorming model that seems most effective for branding is the basic one that most people use, but John Wren of the Idea Café has a counterintuitive rigid style that seems most effective. The following is a set of "rules" for brainstorming that is a blend of Wren's approach and ours:

1. **Select Monitor of the Problem** – This person records suggestions and monitors bursts. We tend to brainstorm on a large flat screen or a whiteboard.

2. **Frame the Problem** – Open forum for questions. Consensus on the problem is established.

3. **Brainstorming Burst** – Ideas must be only one sentence or one breath, whichever comes first. The monitor must record and not respond or comment unless it is to clarify what was said. Questions and responses are strictly forbidden. The monitor decides when a burst is over.

4. **Humor Encouraged** – The best ideas can come from absurd, laughable solutions.

5. **Break When Flow of Ideas Pauses for a Long Time** – Ideas come in bursts. During the break, the monitor reads all of the responses. Participants may record ideas that hitchhike on previous ideas when the next Brainstorming Burst resumes.

6. Burst Repeat – The process can repeat as long as ideas and hitchhikes continue to flow.

7. Ideas are Consolidated – The monitor collects all ideas and e-mails them to all participants so they can go back into the individual creative process for assimilation, or...

8. Addition by Subtraction – For Branding Promise or names a discussion may ensue and then each concept is rated by the group:

    1 = doesn't really work

    2 = OK but not it

    3 = worthy of further consideration

All the 3's are gathered and the discussion and ranking process is done again. You will be surprised at how effective this process is and how concepts seem to change as they proceed through each wave of elimination.

9. Freeze-Ups – When brainstorming sits stymied, take a time out and look at outside stimulators: the thesaurus, name generators on the web, jargon type language books, etc.

10. Simmering Time – After a decision is made all stakeholders should let the concept take hold. After 48 hours, another re-evaluation meeting should be held before proceeding.

As a design firm we use lots of tricks and tactics to stimulate creativity. We keep coming back to the above discipline. It is important to fill every space in order to see patterns and themes emerge. Branding Maps are living, evolving documents that ultimately must knit together to define a strong brand.

Genius Simple Branding At Work

Complete your Branding Map…Create BUZZ to generate sales.

There are two ways to be guided through the Branding Map process:

> **Branding Map Online** - Andy Cleary will guide you through your Branding Lab work book (downloadable) in a nuts and bolts workshop video.

    -Includes GS Brand 360 Diagnostic (8 people)

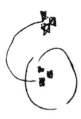

> **Branding Map with a Pro** - Via online teleconferernce or in our "Robot Room" in Denver,Colorado. Call for an appointment.

    - Includes GS go to market strategy.

    - Includes Branding Map Recap and walkthrough.

    - Includes GS Brand 360 Diagnostic (36 people)

For more information and to get started go to:
www.BrandingMap.com

After your Branding Map is complete the next step is...
Genius Simple Design

⟩ **GS Design Online** - All projects GS Branded and Art Directed with GS Certified Designers. You have a Packaged Price Menu for Logo, Business Card, Brochure, Web Site, E-Blast Template. Includes one year of Fast Forward support.

⟩ **GS Design Studio** - Project Based Estimates according to your specific needs.

Preflight planning and full ongoing access to Orbit's Art Director. Project Management and follow through services for your work. Includes on year of Fast Forward support.

For more information go to: **www.GeniusSimpleDesign.com**

303 433-1616
www.orbit-design.com

ORBIT
d e s i g n
Genius Simple Branding™

Name (Handle and Extender)
Slogan (Points towards your separator)
Tag (Rarely used – credibility)

Genius Simple
BRANDING MAP

> TRUE NORTH

Branding Promise: (What do you stand for?)
Vision: (Where are you going?)
Mission: (To support and inspire)
Theme word: (Stakeholders main Value)
URL: (Your main domain and landing pages)
Position/Vertical: (Your "first and only…")

Own Keywords: (Your targeted keywords)

(Note: Your naming structure should follow a
  common theme)
E-Blast name:

Blog name:

Auto-responder name:

Book/Program name:

> ELITE EIGHT

1. (Your top Eight Crowds)
  (List "Influencers" for your number 1 crowd)
2.
3.
4.
5.
6.
7.
8.

VAR (Your value added resellers)

End User Job Title:
Age: Sex: Education:
Groups:
PH Factor-- (Pain/Hunger/Fear):

> BRAND PACKAGE

Apathy Killer: (Your separators: First and only,
pattern interrupting, signature attention getter)

Anchor Benefit: (What keeps them coming back)

Credibility Kicker: (First and only, pattern interrupting,
signature qualification or good works)

Ice Breaker: (Newbie Path)
Branding Icons:
  Spokesperson: (Trusted Advisor or client)
  Animal: (Mascot)
  Toy: (Mascot)

Theme: (Consistent look, feel and tone)
IP: (Program, Book, System, System, Software,
Patent, etc.)
Prop: (Symbolic give-away for shows, speaking)
Color: (Company color theme)

> MESSAGING/DESTINATION

> Salty Sound Bite (storyline): (Salt the listener's
interest and desire to know more)

> Value Prop: (How are you providing extra value in
the transaction)

> Conversation theme: (What is your expertise, your
primary value, or customer relevant subject that is the
basis of an ongoing conversation between you and
your crowd(s)

Sales Model: (Default sales method)

Breakthrough: (What is the next level?)

Next Step: Genius Simple Design & Fast Forward

© 2000-2011 Orbit Design   www.orbit-design.com · 303.433.1616   Validated By:

For the Branding Map Process with a Pro, call **303 433-1616**

For the Branding Map Process online, visit **www.BrandingMap.com**

Conclusion

It is tempting to end this book with a favorite quote, that seems to have been written specifically for and about Genius Simple Branding™:

> *"Whatever you can do or dream you can, begin it. Boldness has genius, power and magic in it."*
> **— Johann Wolfgang von Goethe**

However, two quotes seem apt as you build your branding map:

"If you go to work on your goals, your goals will work on you. If you go to work on your plan, your plan will work on you. Whatever good things we build, end up building us."

> **— Jim Rohn** *(Business Author and Speaker)*

"The way to get started is to quit talking and begin doing."

> **— Walt Disney**

Brand well and prosper!

Your Genius Simple Brand Authors

❭ Andy Cleary – Orbit Design™

Andy Cleary has been involved with writing, design, and marketing for 30 years. After graduating from CU Boulder in English Literature, he started out writing for the *Rocky Mountain News* and the *Denver Post* but soon became interested in commercial writing. He was general manager for two design firms before starting his own company 28 years ago. Orbit Design™ provides professional print and web design services combined with a focus on Genius Simple Branding.™ Andy has developed a trademarked "Branding Map™" process and a book called *Genius Simple Branding™ Workbook* that brings the big business advantage of a cohesive, vital brand to growing businesses.

❭ Cody Cleary

Cody Cleary has been involved with Orbit Design™ as long as he can remember since his father Andy Cleary started the business the same year that Cody was born. After graduating with honors from Trinity University in San Antonio, Texas with a degree in Business and Spanish and a minor in Comparative Literature, Cody went home to Denver for a few years and worked full time for Orbit Design™. He attended the Johnson School of Business at Cornell University in Ithaca, New York earning his MBA in Branding. He won the McAlister Award for Marketing Case Writing and served as a TA in Branding. Cleary is currently employed as a Brand Manager with Colgate Palmolive® in New York City.

Cody edited the client only edition of the Genius Simple Branding™ Workbook and is solely responsible for its final publication by prohibiting his father from making further changes.

Appendix A - Covering Martha's Bases

To hit a home run with Martha you must cover these 7 bases immediately (yes, there are extra bases – remember this is Martha's game not the national past time).

Martha loves:

1. Simplicity – She's already got complicated – that's why she came to you in the first place.

2. Discovery – Be or deliver something new – she loves making a discovery – learning something new – and if you are a good one, she will share you with others.

3. Systems – A reliable, unique system embodied by or behind a product or service can make it irresistible.

4. Credibility – Referrals, endorsements, sanctions, certifications, degrees.

5. Now – The closer to now that you deliver (quote, process, product), the happier she will be.

6. Bargain – Martha is like Donald Trump; they both want a deal – high value to cost ratio. Added value is great. If bargain means "cheap" then you are selling a commodity.

7. Self Actualization – Show Martha her own greatness in your service or product and your sales work is done.

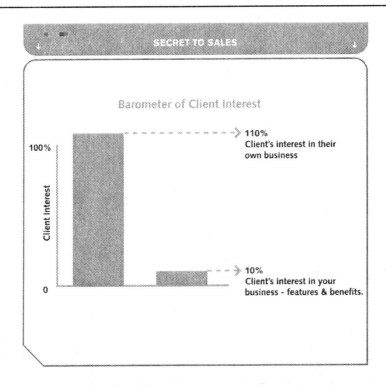

SECRET TO SALES

Barometer of Client Interest

110%
Client's interest in their own business

10%
Client's interest in your business - features & benefits.

100%

Client Interest

0

Recommended Reading List

This list is branding and sales oriented and all are excellent reads. Many must-read general business books like *Think* and *Grow Rich*, *Good to Great* and the *Pursuit of Excellence* are not included but certainly recommended.

The Brand Gap: How to Bridge the Distance Between Business Strategy and Design by Marty Neumeier

Built to Last: Successful Habits of Visionary Companies by James C. Collins and Jerry I. Porras

Buzz: Harness the Power of the Influence and Create Demand by Marian Salzman, Ira Matathia and Ann O'Reilly

The Culture Code: An Ingenious Way to Understand Why People Around the World Live and Buy as They Do by Clotaire Rapaille

The E-Myth Revisited: Why Most Small Businesses Don't Work and What to Do About It by Michael E. Gerber

Marketing Outrageously: How to Increase Your Revenue by Staggering Amounts! by Jon Spoelstra

Marketing Without Advertising: Creative Strategies for Small Business Success by Michael Phillips and Salli Rasberry

Never Eat Alone by Keith Ferrazzi.

The Popcorn Report: Faith Popcorn on the Future of Your Company, Your World, Your Life by Faith Popcorn

Positioning: The Battle for Your Mind by Al Ries and Jack Trout

Selling the Invisible: A Field Guide to Modern Marketing by Harry Beckwith

The Slight Edge: Secret to a Successful Life by Jeff Olson

Streetfighting: Low-Cost Advertising/Promotion Strategies for Your Small Business by Jeff Slutsky and Woody Woodruff

Trademark: How to Name a Business & Product by Kate McGrath and Stephen Elias with Sarah Shena

The Trusted Advisor by David H. Maister, Robert Galford and Charles Green

You Can't Teach a Kid to Ride a Bike at a Seminar: The Sandler Sales Institute's 7-Step System for Successful Selling by David H. Sandler

The Findability Formula by Heather Lutze